n

ner Heide

chwitz

Hosterwitz
Pillnitz

oß–
hachwitz

Müglitz

Pirna *Elbe*

JÜRGEN HELFRICHT

Liebenswertes Dresden

Dresden, close to my heart

TRANSLATED BY JOHN SEWELL

HUSUM

Umschlaggestaltung unter Verwendung von Motiven aus dem Buch

Bibliografische Information der Deutschen Nationalbibliothek

Die Deutsche Nationalbibliothek verzeichnet diese Publikation in der Deutschen Nationalbibliografie; detaillierte bibliografische Daten sind im Internet über http://dnb.d-nb.de abrufbar.

© 2012 by Husum Druck- und Verlagsgesellschaft mbH u. Co. KG, Husum

Gesamtherstellung: Husum Druck- und Verlagsgesellschaft, Postfach 1480, D-25804 Husum – www.verlagsgruppe.de

ISBN 978-3-89876-606-7

Inhalt
Content

Dresden — Europas schönste barocke Stadt
Dresden — Europe's most beautiful Baroque City

Von grünen Hügeln, Wald und Weinbergen umgeben, liegt die über 523 000 Einwohner zählende Hauptstadt des Freistaates Sachsen mit ihrem milden Klima in einem Talkessel der Elbe. Seit Jahrhunderten ist Dresden als barocke Perle, als eine der wichtigsten Städte der Kunst und Kultur Europas berühmt. Johann Gottfried Herder (1747–1803), der Dichter und Philosoph, nannte sie prägnant „Deutsches Florenz", aus dem im Laufe der Zeit „Elbflorenz" wurde.

Die frühesten Ursprünge der Metropole liegen noch im Dunkeln. Wie Wissenschaftler kürzlich herausfanden, könnte Dresden mit dem Ort Lupfurdum identisch sein, den der griechische Gelehrte Claudius Ptolemäus (um 100 – um 160) in seinem Kartenwerk „Geographike Hyphegesis" einzeichnete. Der heutige Name der Stadt ist altsorbischen Ursprungs und leitet sich wohl von „Drezdane" ab (im Wald ansässig gewordene Siedler). In der Kaufmannsniederlassung an einer für den Fernhandel wichtigen Flussquerung errichtete ein Herrscher aus dem Geschlecht der Wettiner vermutlich nach 1144 seine Burg. Diese Familie bestimmte als Markgrafen, Herzöge, Kurfürsten und Könige bis 1918 maßgeblich die Geschicke der Stadt und des Landes.

Erstmals urkundlich erwähnt ist Dresden im Jahre 1206. Wo heute die Augustusbrücke die Elbe überquert, befand sich 1285 schon eine aus Stein gemauerte Brücke. Mit 24 Bögen, 561 Meter Länge und 8,5 Meter Breite gehörte sie zu den größten Brücken im damaligen Europa. Als Sachsens Herrscher im Jahre 1485 ihren Hofstaat von Meißen nach Dresden verlegten, erlangte die Stadt Residenzstatus. Während der Renaissance um 1600 wohnten hier rund 15 000 Einwohner. Zu jener Zeit wurde das Stadtbild

Surrounded by green hills, forests and vineyards, the capital of Saxony, with over 523 000 inhabitants and enjoying a mild climate, lies in the Elbe valley. For centuries Dresden, the Baroque pearl, has been renowned as one of Europe's most important cities of art and culture. Johann Gottfried Herder (1747–1803), poet and philosopher, aptly called it "German Florence" which in the course of time became the "Florence of the north."

The earliest origins of the city are still unclear. As scientists recently discovered, the location of Dresden could have been identical to the place called Lupfurdum, which the Greek scholar Claudius Ptolemaus (circa 100–160) marked on his map, the "Geographike Hyphegesis". The current name of the city is of old Sorbian origin and probably derived from "Drezdane" (settlers who became established in the forest). Performing the duties of a clerk of an important river crossing for long-distance trade, a ruler from the House of Wettin built his castle here probably after 1144. Significant for the fortunes of the city and state were the members of this family, who were appointed as margraves, dukes, elector princes and kings right up to 1918.

The first official recording of Dresden was in 1206. In 1285 a stone built bridge was already in existence where the Augustus Bridge crosses the Elbe today. Consisting of 24 arches, 561 meters long and 8.5 meters wide, it was one of the largest bridges in Europe at that time. As a result of Saxony's ruler moving his entourage from Meissen to Dresden in 1485, the city gained residence status. In 1600, during the Renaissance, about 15,000 inhabitants lived here. At that time, the skyline of the city was dominated by several church towers (for example the Church of the Cross on

von mehreren Kirchtürmen (z. B. der Kreuzkirche am Altmarkt), den nach italienisch-niederländischem Vorbild entstandenen Befestigungswerken und der Vierflügel-Schlossanlage dominiert. Ein herausragender Künstler war damals der aus Lugano in der Schweiz stammende Bildhauer Giovanni Maria Nosseni (1544–1620), den Kurfürst August (1526–1586) im Jahre 1575 nach Dresden berief.

Der Ausbau zur europäischen Residenz von Rang erfolgte im sogenannten Augusteischen Zeitalter – der Regierung von Kurfürst Friedrich August I. (1670–1733, „August der Starke") und seines Sohnes August II. (1696–1763). Beide Sachsen-Herrscher, die auch Könige von Polen waren, füllten ihre Schatzkammer Grünes Gewölbe mit wertvollsten Preziosen, bauten eine einzigartige Gemäldesammlung auf und beschäftigten Stäbe von Architekten und Steinbildhauern aus ganz Europa. Besonders erwähnenswert sind neben Johann Christoph Knöffel (1686–1752), Balthasar Permoser (1651–1732) und Matthäus Daniel Pöppelmann (1662–1736) die Franzosen Jean de Bodt (1670–1745) und Zacharias Longuelune (1669–1748) oder die Italiener Gaetano Chiaveri (1689– 1770) und Lorenzo Mattielli (1688–1748). Von ih-

the Altmarkt), the fortifications designed after Italian-Dutch examples and also the four-wing castle. An outstanding artist of that time was the sculptor Giovanni Maria Nosseni (1544–1620), from Lugano in Switzerland who was summoned to Dresden by the Elector Prince August (1526–1586) in 1575.

The extension to the distinguished European residence was made in the so-called Augustan age – the reign of Prince Elector Friedrich August I (1670–1733), colloquially known as "August the Strong", and his son August II (1696–1763). Both Saxon rulers, who were also kings of Poland, filled their Green Vault treasure chamber with precious gems, founded a unique collection of paintings and commissioned architects and stone masons from all over Europe. Particularly noteworthy are, besides Johann Christoph Knöffel (1686–1752), Balthasar Permoser (1651–1732) and Matthew Daniel Pöppelmann (1662–1736), the Frenchmen Jean de Bodt (1670–1745) and Zacharias Longuelune (1669–1748) and the Italians Chiaveri Gaetano (1689–1770) and Lorenzo Mattielli (1688–1748). It is thanks to them that Dresden is blessed today with such imposing structures such as the Zwinger, the Japanese Palace, Schloss Pillnitz, their summer castle, the Taschenberg Palace and the Catholic Cathe-

So sah der Zeichner Wilhelm Dilich Dresden im Jahre 1650.

This is how the draughtsman Wilhelm Dilich depicted Dresden in 1650.

nen erhielten sich bis heute imposante Bauwerke wie Zwinger, Japanisches Palais, Schloss Pillnitz, Taschenbergpalais oder Hofkirche. Etwa zur gleichen Zeit schuf der geniale George Bähr (1661–1738) mit der Frauenkirche die prachtvollste Kathedrale der evangelischen Christenheit. Viele dieser Wunder der Baukunst malte der Venezianer Bernardo Bellotto, genannt Canaletto (1721–1780), in seinen Veduten. Auch ein Landsmann, der Abenteurer und Schriftsteller Giacomo Girolamo Casanova (1725–1798), hielt sich damals in Dresden auf. Seine Mutter wirkte hier als Schauspielerin, seine Schwester als Tänzerin. Casanovas Bruder Giovanni Battista (1730–1795) wurde sogar Rektor der Kunstakademie.

Der von Preußen aufgezwungene Siebenjährige Krieg (1756–1763) zerrüttete Sachsens Wirtschaft und Finanzen. 1760 fiel die Hälfte der Dresdner Altstadt einem Bombardement zum Opfer. Weitere Zeiten des Elends folgten, als das junge Königreich Sachsen 1813 an der Seite Napoleon Bonapartes (1769–1821), der mehrfach in Dresden weilte, den Krieg verlor. Fortan bestimmte der russische Fürst Nikolai von Repnin-Wolkonski (1778–1845) als Generalgouverneur die Geschicke des Landes, das nach dem Wiener Kongress 1815 die Hälfte seines Territoriums an Preußen verlor. Ihm verdankt Dresden den Wiederaufbau des Parkareals Großer Garten. Und er ließ die Freitreppe zur Brühlschen Terrasse anlegen, die dadurch zur Flaniermeile, zum „Balkon Europas", wurde.

Dieses wunderschöne Dresden musste man gesehen, mindestens einmal besucht haben. Der polnische Komponist Frédéric Chopin (1810–1849) schuf hier seinen „Abschiedswalzer", der russische Romancier Fjodor Michailowitsch Dostojewski (1821–1881) weilte 25 Monate in der Stadt, der dänische Märchenerzähler Hans Christian Andersen (1805–1875) kam sogar 32 Mal!

Ein Baukünstler, der sich an der italienischen Hochrenaissance orientierte, drückte der Stadt besonders seinen Stempel auf: Gottfried Semper (1803–1879)! Zu seinen Werken gehören die den Zwinger nördlich abschließende Gemäldegalerie und das

dral, formerly the Court Church. About the same time the brilliant architect George Bähr (1661–1738) created the Frauenkirche (Church of Our Lady), the most magnificent cathedral of the Lutheran faith. The Venetian Bernardo Bellotto called Canaletto (1721–1780) captured many of these architectural wonders in his vista paintings. Even a compatriot, the adventurer and writer Giacomo Girolamo Casanova (1725–1798), resided in Dresden at that time. His mother worked there as an actress, his sister as a dancer. Casanova's brother Giovanni Battista (1730–1795) was even president of the Academy of Art.

The Seven Years War (1756–1763), forced upon Dresden by the Prussians, wrecked Saxon's economy and finances. Half of the Dresden's Altstadt fell victim to the bombing of 1760. Other periods of misery followed when the young kingdom of Saxony lost the war in 1813 as a result of siding with Napoleon Bonaparte (1769–1821), who stayed in Dresden on several occasions. Henceforth, the Russian Prince Nikolai Repnin-Wolkonski (1778–1845) acting as Governor-General determined the fortunes of the country which, after the Congress of Vienna in 1815, lost half of its territory to Prussia. Dresden owes to him the reconstruction of the Grosser Garten parklands and also the construction of the staircase to the Brühl Terrace, which resulted in the promenade known as the "Balcony of Europe".

One must see this beautiful city of Dresden and have visited it at least once in one's lifetime. The Polish composer Frederic Chopin (1810–1849) composed his "Farewell Waltz" here, the Russian novelist Fyodor Mikhailovich Dostoyevsky (1821–1881) stayed here for 25 months, the Danish storyteller Hans Christian Andersen (1805–1875) even paid 32 visits.

Inspired by the Italian Renaissance, Gottfried Semper (1803–1879) was the architect who left a very special mark on the city. Among his works are the Gemäldegalerie Alte Meister (Gallery of the Old Masters) closing the northern section of the Zwinger and the Royal Court Theatre (now called the Semper Opera House) on Theatre Square. Semper, who was involved in the building of the barri-

königliche Hoftheater (heute Semperoper genannt) am Theaterplatz. In den Wirren der Revolution von 1848/49, die z. B. auch den russischen Anarchisten Michail Bakunin (1814–1876) nach Dresden verschlugen, musste der am Bau von Barrikaden beteiligte „Hochverräter" Semper aus dem Lande fliehen.

Das 19. Jahrhundert – im letzten Drittel erlebte Dresden den rasanten Aufschwung zur Großstadt mit mehr als 300 000 Einwohnern – prägten nicht nur imposante Schlösser am Elbhang, die Um- und Neubauten auf der Brühlschen Terrasse sowie die gegenüberliegenden Ministerien. Dresden wurde auch ein wichtiger Fremdenverkehrsort und zeitweilige Heimat von Menschen aus aller Welt. Hier ließen sich z. B. der russische Fürst Nikolaus Abramowitsch Putjatin (1749–1830), sein Landsmann, der Komponist und Pianist Anton Rubinstein (1829–1896), der italienische Magier Bartolomeo Bosco (1793–1863) oder der polnische Schriftsteller Josef Ignacy Kraszewski (1812–1887) nieder. Es gründeten sich sogar eigenständige Ausländer-Gemeinden, die nahe dem Hauptbahnhof Kirchen errichteten: 1869 die englische Kirche All Saints, 1874 die russisch-orthodoxe Kirche des Heiligen Simeon vom wunderbaren Berge, 1883 die amerikanische Kirche St. John und 1884 eine schottisch-presbyterianische Kirche.

cades, was a "traitor" who had to flee the country during the turmoil of the revolution of 1848/49 when also, amongst others, the Russian anarchist Michail Bakunin (1814–1876) came to Dresden.
The 19th century, in which Dresden experienced a rapid economic boom, thus becoming a capital city with over 300 000 inhabitants, was not only marked by imposing castles on the Elbe slopes, but also the renovations and new constructions on Brühl Terrace as well as the ministry buildings on the opposite shore of the Elbe river. Dresden also became an important tourist centre and a temporary home for people from all over the world. The Russian Prince Nikolaus Abramowitsch Putjatin (1749–1830), his compatriot, the composer and pianist Anton Rubinstein (1829–1896), the Italian magician Bartolomeo Bosco (1793–1863) and the Polish writer Josef Ignacy Kraszewski (1812–1887) all settled here. There were even founded independent foreign communities who established their churches near the main railway station: in 1869 the English All Saints Church, in 1874 the Russian Orthodox Church of Saint Simeon, in 1883 the American Saint John's Church and in 1884 a Scottish Presbyterian Church.
In the picturesque city of Dresden, where European porcelain and that most famous of German Christmas cakes, the original Dresden Christstollen, saw the light of

Kurfürst Friedrich August I. von Sachsen war auch König von Polen. Gemälde von Louis de Silvestre, um 1718

Elector Frederick August I of Saxony was also King of Poland. Painting by Louis de Silvestre, about 1718

Im malerischen Dresden, wo Europas Porzellan und das berühmteste deutsche Weihnachtsgebäck – der Original Dresdner Christstollen – das Licht der Welt erblickten, erfand man auch die Milchschokolade, das künstliche Mineralwasser, die Kondensmilch, den Kaffeefilter, das erste Mundwasser, die Schuhcreme in der Tube, die Zahnpastatube, den Teebeutel, den Büstenhalter und die Spiegelreflexkamera. Lange vor dem Ersten Weltkrieg erblühten hier Mittelstand und Industrie. Zum Wahrzeichen der Macht eines Zigaretten-Großunternehmers wurde 1908/09 der

day, milk chocolate, artificial mineral water, evaporated milk, the coffee filter, the first mouthwash, shoe polish in the tube, the toothpaste tube, the tea bag, the brassiere and the SLR camera also had their origins here. Long before the First World War, both the middle class as well as industry flourished. The construction of the Yenidze Tabakkontor, an industrial building, in 1908/09, whose design was modelled after a mosque, was a symbol of the power of a cigarette manufacturer. It became a focal point for discussions concerning architectural reforms and Art Nouveau. Exemplary

Der barocke Neumarkt mit der Frauenkirche, Gemälde von Bernardo Bellotto, 1749/1751

The Baroque Neumarkt with the Frauenkirche, painted by Bernardo Bellotto in 1749/1751

Dresden um 1911, aquarellierte Zeichnung von Adolph Michalsky

Dresden (circa 1911), watercolour painting by Adolph Michalsky

Industriebau der Yenidze, welcher einer Moschee nachempfunden ist. Dieser sorgte damals genauso für Diskussionen wie Reformarchitektur und Jugendstil. Mustergültig war ab 1908 der Bau der ersten deutschen Gartenstadtsiedlung Hellerau für Arbeiter der Deutschen Werkstätten im Dresdner Norden.

Mit der Abdankung des letzten Königs, Friedrich August III. (1865–1932), verlor Dresden den Rang einer Residenz, blieb jedoch Verwaltungszentrum des Freistaates Sachsen. Durch Eingemeindung zahlreicher Dörfer entstand bis zum Zweiten Weltkrieg eine Metropole, die mit 649 252 Menschen im Jahre 1933 zu den fünf größten Städten Deutschlands zählte. Unter der Nazi-Herrschaft, deren wahres Gesicht sich spätestens in den Exzessen der Reichskristallnacht vom 9./10. November 1938 zeigte – in

was also the construction in 1908 of the first German garden city of Hellerau in the north of Dresden, comprising settlements for the workers of the German Werkstätten (studios and workshops). With the abdication of the last Saxon king, Friedrich August III. (1865–1932), and the rise of the National Socialists, Dresden was no longer entitled to call itself a Residence City, remained, however, the administrative centre of Saxony. A metropolis which numbered 649,252 inhabitants in 1933 was formed by the incorporation of numerous villages and was, up to the time of the Second World War, one of the five largest cities in Germany. Particularly the Jewish population suffered terribly under the National Socialist regime, which finally showed its true colours in the excesses of the Reichskristallnacht ("Scherbennacht", night of the

Luftbildaufnahme des alten Dresner Stadtzentrums vor 1945

Aerial photograph of the old Dresden city centre before 1945

dieser Nacht wurde auch die Synagoge Gottfried Sempers vernichtet – mussten besonders die Juden leiden. Vor allem durch Auswanderung und Deportation in Vernichtungslager verringerte sich die Zahl der Mitglieder der jüdischen Gemeinde von 4397 im Jahre 1933 auf etwa 70 zum Kriegsende.

broken glass) of 9th to 10th November 1938, in which also Gottfried Semper's Synagogue in Dresden was destroyed. The number of members of the Jewish community in Dresden decreased from 4397 in 1933 to about 70 by the end of the war especially due to emigration and the deportation to concentration camps.

Die Innenstadt war nach dem Bombardement vom 13./14. Februar 1945 auf 15 Quadratkilometern völlig zerstört.

A 15 square kilometer area of the inner-city was totally desfroyed after the arial bombardment of 13th to 14th February 1945

Als einzige große deutsche Stadt bis kurz vor Kriegsende nahezu unversehrt geblieben, erlitt Dresden in der Nacht vom 13. zum 14. Februar 1945 ein Flächenbombardement von 772 englischen und 311 US-Flugzeugen. 3500 Tonnen Bomben ließen über 25 000 Menschen sterben. Sie verbrannten auf offener Straße, wurden

Dresden, the only major German city until shortly before the end of the war to have remained virtually unscathed, suffered aerial carpet bombardment by 772 British and 311 US aircrafts on the night of 13th to 14th February 1945. 3500 tons of bombs left over 25 000 people dead. They burnt to death in the streets, were

von einstürzenden Häusern erschlagen, von Tieffliegern erschossen, erstickten in Kellern. Die tragischste Zäsur der Stadtgeschichte überlebte in einem Keller des Schlachthofes der junge amerikanische Kriegsgefangene Kurt Vonnegut (1922–2007). Das Inferno verarbeitete er später in seinem Erfolgsroman „Schlachthof 5".

Der Neuanfang begann nach 1945 unter den kommunistischen Stadtverwaltern, denen im Elbtal eine „sozialistische Großstadt" vorschwebte. Dem Abbruchvandalismus in der DDR mussten u. a. die gotische Sophienkirche und ganze historische Straßenzüge weichen, aber die Aura der Kunst- und Kulturstadt konnten sie nicht auslöschen. Denkmalschützer und Architekten sicherten viele Ruinen für spätere Zeiten, sorgten z. B. bis 1985 für den Wiederaufbau der Semperoper.

Im Herbst 1989 verjagte die friedliche Revolution die alten Machthaber. 1994 erfolgte der Abzug der sowjetischen Besatzer (im Raum Dresden war die 1. Gardepanzerarmee stationiert), für deren Geheimdienst KGB der heutige russische Präsident Wladimir Putin (geb. 1952) bis zum Zusammenbruch der DDR fünf Jahre lang in Dresden gearbeitet hatte.

Nach dem Zusammenschluss beider deutscher Staaten, welcher 1990 die Wiedergründung des Freistaates Sachsen mit Dresden als Landeshauptstadt ermöglichte, stoppten Aufbau-Milliarden und viele private Investoren den Verfall der historischen Substanz und sorgten dafür, dass die Stadt wieder in alter Pracht entsteht. Eine weltweite Bürgerinitiative machte den Wiederaufbau der Frauenkirche (2005) möglich. Um das Gotteshaus entstand der Neumarkt mit historisierenden Fassaden. Das Residenzschloss soll 2015 fertig sein. Daneben wurden moderne Gebäude wie der Landtag, die Neue Synagoge, die Staats- und Universitätsbibliothek oder das Kongresszentrum errichtet. Mit dem Militärhistorischen Museum der Bundeswehr (2011) gelang zuletzt dem US-Architekten Daniel Libeskind (geb. 1946) die Symbiose von Alt und Neu.

killed by collapsing houses, suffocated in cellars and perished from the attacks by strafing bombers. The young American POW Kurt Vonnegut (1922–2007) survived the most tragic turning point of the city's history in a cellar of the city's slaughterhouse. Later he assimilated his experience of the inferno in his successful novel "Slaughterhouse-Five".

After 1945 the city's newstart began under the communist city administration, who were determined to build a "socialist capital" in the Elbe valley. The Gothic Church of St. Sophia and whole quarters of historic streets had to yield to the GDR's wanton demolition, but the aura of art and culture of the city could not be extinguished. Preservationists and architects secured many of the ruins for later times, and saw to it until 1985 that, for example, the Semper Opera House was rebuilt. The peaceful revolution of autumn 1989 drove out the old rulers. 1994 saw the withdrawal of the Soviet occupation force (the 1st Guard's Tank Army was stationed in the Dresden area), for whose KGB secret service the Russian President Vladimir Putin (born in 1952) worked in Dresden for five years until the collapse of the GDR.

Following the merger of the two German states, which in 1990 made possible the re-establishment of the Free State of Saxony with Dresden as the state capital, countless billions of construction funds and a flood of private investors checked the decline of the historic fabric and made sure that the city could win back its former glory. A global citizen initiative made the rebuilding of the Frauenkirche (completed in 2005) possible. With its historicist facades the Neumarkt presents a fitting backdrop for the magnificent church. In addition, modern buildings such as the Parliament, the new Synagogue, the State and University Library and the Convention Centre can now be admired while the completion of the Residence Castle is to be expected in 2015. U.S. architect Daniel Libeskind (born 1946), has recently achieved a successful symbiosis of old and new with the 2011 reconstruction of the German Bundeswehr's Museum of Military History.

Diese Panoramasicht nach Norden umfasst große Teile des historischen Stadtkerns. Vom linken Bildrand mit dem Ensemble von Residenzschloss und Hofkirche reicht sie über den Neumarkt mit der Frauenkirche bis zur gläsernen Kuppel der Kunstakademie, im Vordergrund Häuser um die Wilsdruffer Straße.

This panoramic view to the north includes large parts of the historic city centre. From the left side of the picture with the ensemble of the Residence Castle and the Catholic Cathedral (no longer officially called the Court Church) it continues to the Neumarkt with the Frauenkirche all the way to the glass dome of the Academy of Fine Arts, with the buildings along Wilsdrufferstrasse in the foreground.

Nordöstlicher Blick vom Rathausturm auf das Herz Dresdens: die Kreuzkirche mit kupfergrünem Dach und 94 Meter hohem Turm sowie die den Altmarkt umgebenden Gebäude. Von hier aus entwickelte sich die mittelalterliche Stadt zur heutigen Metropole mit 523 000 Einwohnern.

North-eastern view from the City Hall Tower toward the heart of Dresden, taking in the Kreuzkirche (Church of the Cross) with its copper green roof and 94 meter high tower, as well as the buildings surrounding the Altmarkt. This is where the medieval town began to develop into today's metropolis of 523 000 inhabitants.

Von der Pantherquadriga der Semperoper über dem Theaterplatz mit Reiterstandbild von König Johann (1801–1873) sehen wir auf das im Verlauf der Jahrhunderte immer wieder umgebaute Residenzschloss mit dem Hausmannsturm und die 1980 zur Kathedrale Sanctissimae Trinitatis erhobene Katholische Hofkirche.

From the Pantherquadriga (a chariot pulled by four panthers) on the roof of the Semper Opera House we have a view over Theatre Square, taking in the equestrian statue of King Johann (1801–1873), the Residence Castle with the Hausmann Tower, which has been rebuilt again and again over the course of centuries and the Court Church, which was raised to the status of a Cathedral Sanctissimae Trinitatus in 1980.

Westseite des Dresdner Residenzschlosses, wie sie sich seit dem Umbau anlässlich des 800-jährigen Jubiläums des Königshauses 1889 zeigt. Bis 1918 war das Schloss nahe der Elbe Wohnsitz der sächsischen Herrscher aus dem Hause Wettin, Macht- und Regierungszentrum des Landes.

The west side of the reconstructed Dresden Residence Castle, as it looked on the occasion of the 800-year anniversary of the royal family in 1889. Until 1918 the castle was the residence of the Saxon rulers of the House of Wettin, and also the governmental seat and centre of Saxony.

Der große Schlosshof des Residenzschlosses zeigt sich heute wieder in der künstlerischen Ausgestaltung der Renaissance. Damals wurden die bedeutendsten Architekten und Künstler Europas wie der Italiener Francesco Ricchino an den Fürsten-Hof geholt, die Fassaden mittels Sgraffito-Technik verziert.

Today again the large courtyard of the Residence Castle displays the artistic décor of the Renaissance. At that time the most famous architects and artists in Europe as for example the Italian Francesco Ricchino, were summoned to the prince's court in order to restore and decorate the facades in the sgraffito technique.

Türklopfer einer Stahltür im Schlosshof. Der junge Löwe hält einen zur Schlange geformten Ring im Maul. Nach alter Vorstellung ist der Löwe als Wächter besonders geeignet, weil er sogar beim Schlafen die Augen offen hält. Die Symbolsprache geht bis auf die Bibel zurück, in der Jesus sagt: „Klopfet an! So wird euch aufgetan!"

A steel door knocker in the castle courtyard. The young lion is holding a serpent-shaped ring in its jaws. According to old legends, the lion is particularly suitable as a guard, because it keeps its eyes open even when sleeping. The symbolism goes back to the Bible, where Jesus says: "Knock! And the door will be opened!"

Rechts: Blick vom großen Schlosshof auf den Hausmannsturm. Der 100,7 Meter hohe Turm ist das Wahrzeichen des Schlosses. Kurz vor 1400 entstanden, gehört er zu den ältesten Teilen des Gebäude-Ensembles. Wer die 222 Stufen erklimmt, hat aus 68 Meter Höhe einen traumhaften Blick über die Dächer von Dresden.

Above right: View from the large courtyard towards the Hausmann Tower. The 100.7-meter-high tower is the emblem of the castle. It was erected shortly before 1400 and is one of the oldest parts of the building complex. Those who climb the 222 steps to a height of 68 metres can enjoy a breathtaking view over the rooftops of Dresden.

„Hofstaat zu Delhi am Geburtstag des Großmoguls Aurang-Zeb": Dieser goldene Traum von Indien umfasst heute noch 132 Figuren, die u. a. mit 4909 Diamanten, 160 Rubinen, 164 Smaragden und 16 Perlen verziert sind. Hofjuwelier Johann Melchior Dinglinger (1664 – 1731) schuf ihn 1701/1709. Das Prachtstück gehört zu 1089 Kunstwerken, die in zehn Räumen des ersten Obergeschosses (Westflügel) im Neuen Grünen Gewölbe gezeigt werden.

Court of Delhi on the occasion of the birthday of the Grand Mogul Aurang Zeb". This golden dream of India today still consists of 132 figures decorated with 4909 diamonds, 160 rubies, 164 emeralds and 16 pearls. Court Jeweller Johann Melchior Dinglinger (1664–1731) created this in 1701/1709. The showpiece is one of 1089 works of art that are displayed in ten rooms on the first floor (west wing) of the New Green Vault.

Linke Seite: Eine der reichsten Schatzkammern Europas ist das Grüne Gewölbe (hier das Juwelenzimmer im historischen Teil). August der Starke schuf 1723 bis 1730 im Erdgeschoss des Westflügels seines Schlosses dieses Museum für die größten Kostbarkeiten seines Staatsschatzes. Seit 2006 werden in den barocken Räumen hinter meterdicken Mauern mit höchsten Sicherheitsstandards wieder etwa 3000 Kleinodien von Milliardenwert präsentiert.

Left side: One of the richest treasure chambers of Europe is the Green Vault (here the jewel room in the historic part of the castle). From 1723 to 1730 August the Strong created this museum on the ground floor of the west wing of his castle to house his most precious state treasures. Since 2006, about 3000 valuable gems of priceless value have again been put on display in the Baroque rooms behind meter-thick walls to ensure the highest security standards.

600 Exponate aus dem Osmanenreich zeigt die „Türckische Cammer". Die 1591 von Sachsens Kurfürsten begonnene Sammlung zeigt neben Waffen, Kostümen und Zaumzeugen auf Araberhengsten auch ein großes Staatszelt, das von drei kunstvoll geschnitzten Masten gehalten wird (zwanzig Meter lang, acht Meter breit, sechs Meter hoch). Dieses wurde 1683 vor Wien erbeutet. In Dresden gab es zur Barockzeit auch einen über die Landesgrenzen hinaus berühmten Türkischen Garten mit Palais.

The "Turkish Chamber" displays 600 exhibits from the Ottoman Empire. The collection begun by Saxony's princes in 1591 displays not only weapons, costumes and trappings of Arab stallions but also a large municipal tent (20 meters long, 8 meters wide and 6 meters tall) supported by three ornately carved masts. This was captured at the gates of Vienna in 1683. There was also a famous Turkish garden and palace in Dresden during the Baroque period renowned far beyond the borders of Saxony.

„Englische Treppe", das barocke Pracht-Treppenhaus. Hofbaumeister Johann Georg Starcke (um 1640–1695) konstruierte die über vier Pfeiler geführte Treppe 1692. Ihren Namen verdankt sie einer Auszeichnung des Kurfürsten Johann Georg IV. (1668–1694). Dieser wurde im Jahre 1693 durch den englischen Gesandten Sir William Swan zum Ritter des englischen Hosenbandordens – einem der exklusivsten Orden Großbritanniens (gestiftet 1348) – ernannt.

The splendid Baroque staircase is known as "The English Staircase". Court architect Johann Georg Starcke (circa 1640–1695) constructed the staircase, which is supported by four columns in 1692. It derives its name from a distinction bestowed upon Prince Johann Georg IV. (1668–1694) received when British Ambassador Sir William Swan appointed him Knight of the British Order of the Garter, one of the most exclusive decorations of Great Britain (founded in 1348) in 1693.

Das mit dem Schloss durch einen Gang verbundene Taschenbergpalais bei Nacht. August der Starke ließ diesen 48 Meter langen Bau mit Mansardendach für seine Mätresse Gräfin Cosel (1680 – 1765) errichten. Von 1719 bis zum Anfang des 20. Jahrhunderts wohnte hier die Familie des jeweiligen Kronprinzen. 1991/94 wurde es als „Grandhotel Taschenbergpalais Kempinski Dresden" (182 Zimmer, 32 Suiten) zu einem der bekanntesten Luxushotels Deutschlands wieder aufgebaut. Heute steigen hier Staatschefs, Königinnen, Klassik- und Popstars ab.

The Taschenberg Palais, which is connected to the Castle by a passageway, at night. August the Strong had this 48 meter long structure with the mansard roof built for his mistress, the Countess Cosel (1680-1765). The family respective its descendants of the Crown Prince lived here from 1719 to the early 20th century. From 1991 to 1994 it was rebuilt as the Dresden Taschenbergpalais Kempinski Hotel (182 rooms, 32 suites) since having become one of the most famous luxury hotels in Germany. Today, the hotel accommodates heads of state, royalty, stars of the classics and Pop.

Übergang vom Schloss zur Katholischen Hofkirche. 1761 verband man das Audienzzimmer des Kurfürsten im Nordflügel mittels einer geschlossenen Holz-Brücke mit den königlichen Oratorien der Hofkirche. 1897 wurde diese Brücke durch den heutigen kupfergetriebenen Übergang ersetzt.

Crossing from the Castle to the Catholic Cathedral. In 1761 the elector's audience chamber, located in the north wing, was connected to the royal oratorios in the Court Church by means of an enclosed wooden bridge. This bridge was replaced by today's copper embossed crossing in 1897.

Seit 2012 beherbergt das Grandhotel eine eigene russisch-orthodoxe Kirche, die dem Heiligen Apostel und Fürsten Wladimir, dem Täufer Russlands, geweiht ist. Sie entstand im etwa neun Meter hohen und 108 Quadratmeter großen Saal der ehemaligen katholischen Hauskapelle der Wettiner.

The grand hotel has housed its own Russian Orthodox Church which is dedicated to the Holy Apostle and Prince Vladimir, the Russian Baptist, since 2012. It is situated in the salon (9 meters high x 108 meters in area) which was formerly the Catholic chapel of the Wettin Royal Family.

Wie ein Schiff steht Sachsens größtes katholisches Gotteshaus mit dem 86 Meter hohen Turm am Ufer der Elbe (rechts dahinter die Semperoper). Seit über 250 Jahren feiern hier Christen die Heilige Messe. Kurfürst Friedrich August II. (1696–1763) und seine Gemahlin Maria Josepha Erzherzogin von Österreich (1699–1757) beauftragten 1738 den italienischen Architekten Gaetano Chiaveri (1689–1770) mit dem Bau der 4792 Quadratmeter umfassenden Kirche zwischen Brücke und Residenzschloss im Stil des römischen Spätbarock. Noch unfertig, wurde die Kirche 1751 geweiht.

Saxony's largest Catholic Church with its 86m high tower appears like a ship on the banks of the Elbe (Semper Opera House in the background to the right). Christians have been celebrating Holy Mass here for over 250 years. Elector Friedrich August II (1696–1763) and his wife Maria Josepha, Archduchess of Austria (1699–1757), commissioned the Italian architect Gaetano Chiaveri (1689–1770) with the design and construction of the 4792 square meters church situated between the bridge and the royal palace in the style of the late Roman Baroque period in 1738. Still unfinished, the church was consecrated in 1751.

Blick auf die Balustraden der Hofkirche mit ihrem reichen Figurenschmuck, die Elbe und die gegenüberliegende Dresdner Neustadt. Der in Vicenza geborene und in Dresden gestorbene italienische Bildhauer Lorenzo Mattielli (1688–1748) schuf die 78 überlebensgroßen Heiligenfiguren aus Sandstein der Sächsischen Schweiz.

View of the balustrades of the Court Church with its rich decorative figures, the Elbe River and the Dresden Neustadt on the opposite shore. The Italian sculptor Lorenzo Mattielli (1688–1748), who was born in Vicenza and died in Dresden, created the 78 larger than life figures of the saints from the sandstone of Saxon Switzerland.

Auch der 1669 heiliggesprochene Bußprediger Petrus von Alcantara (1499–1562) schaut vom Dach der Hofkirche. Der franziskanische Ordens-Reformator hat einen Rosenkranz bei sich und gilt als Schutzpatron Brasiliens und Beschützer der Nachtwächter,.

The penitential preacher Peter of Alcantara (1499–1562) canonised in 1669, also looks down from the roof of the Cathedral. The Franciscan Order-reformer, who is holding a rosary, is the patron saint of Brazil and protector of night watchmen.

Über 47 Register auf drei Manualen und etwa 3000 Pfeifen verfügt die größte und letzte Orgel des sächsischen Meisters Gottfried Silbermann (1683–1753). Sie wurde 1755 in der Hofkirche geweiht.

The largest organ and the last one built by the Saxon master organ builder Gottfried Silbermann (1683–1753) has over 47 stops on three manuals and about 3000 pipes. It was consecrated in the Court Church in 1755.

Das 52 Meter lange und 18 Meter breite Hauptschiff der Katholischen Hofkirche, Kathedrale Sanctissimae Trinitatis. Den Hochaltar schmückt das zehn Meter hohe Gemälde „Himmelfahrt Christi", welches erst 1765 per Schiff in Dresden eintraf. Anton Raffael Mengs (1728–1779) hatte es in Rom gemalt und in Madrid vollendet. Die massiv silbernen Leuchter (je 2,15 Meter hoch) und das 4,20 Meter hohe Altar-Kreuz fertigte Ignaz Bauer in Augsburg.

The 52 meter long and 18 meter wide main nave of the Catholic Cathedral Sanctissimae Trinitatis, the former court church. The high altar is decorated with the ten-meter high painting "The Ascension", which arrived in Dresden by ship in 1765. Anton Raphael Mengs (1728–1779) had begun painting it in Rome and completed it in Madrid. The massive silver candlesticks (each 2.15 meters high) and the 4.20 meters high altar cross were created by Ignaz Bauer in Augsburg.

1530/35 errichtete man das Georgentor, welches den Nordflügel des Schlosses mit dem Stallhof verbindet und die Durchfahrt zur Schlossstraße ermöglicht. Das heutige Erscheinungsbild mit steilem Dach, Türmchen, Reliefschmuck und drei Portalen im Stil der Neurenaissance geht auf den Schlossumbau 1900/01 zurück.

The Georgentor (George's gate), which was erected between 1530 and 1535, connects the north wing of the castle with the Royal Mews and allows access to Schlossstrasse (Castle Street). Today's appearance with the steep roof, turrets, relief decorations and three portals in the neo-Renaissance style is the result of the 1900–01 reconstruction.

Prunksarg von König Johann (1801–1873). In den Grüften der Hofkirche befindet sich die wichtigste Grablege des sächsischen Fürsten- und Königshauses Wettin, welches durch seine Heirats-Politik mit vielen Herrschergeschlechtern Europas verwandt ist. Vom berühmtesten aller Sachsen-Monarchen, August dem Starken, ist nur das Herz in einer silbernen Kapsel vorhanden. Sein Leib ruht in der Königsgruft auf dem Wawel im polnischen Krakau.

The magnificent coffin of King Johann (1801–1873). In the crypts of the Court Church are found the most important burial sites of the Saxon princes and of the Royal House of Wettin which, through its marriage policy, is related to many European dynasties. Enclosed in a silver capsule, the heart is all that exists of the most famous of all the Saxon monarchs, August the Strong. His body rests in the royal crypt on the Wawel Mount in Cracow, Poland.

Die Schlossstraße mit dem Hauptportal des Residenzschlosses (rechts) gehörte zu den vornehmsten Straßen Dresdens. Natürlich hatte einst auch die Königliche und später Staatliche Porzellanmanufaktur Meissen® hier ihre Hauptfiliale in der Landeshauptstadt. Touristen gelangen von dieser Straße in den überdachten kleinen Schlosshof, von dem aus alle Museen in diesem Komplex erreichbar sind.

Schlossstrasse with the main portal to the Residence Castle once was one of the most elegant streets of Dresden. It goes without saying that the Royal and later state-owned Meissen porcelain® manufactory also had their headquarters in the Saxon capital right here. From this street tourists can enter the small castle courtyard, from where all the museums in this complex may be accessed.

35 sächsische Markgrafen, Herzöge, Kurfürsten und Könige aus dem Hause Wettin sind an der Nordwand des „Langen Ganges" am Stallhof (Augustusstraße) abgebildet. Bei dem 1907 fertiggestellten Fürstenzug handelt es sich um das weltgrößte Porzellanwandbild aus 25 000 fugenlos in Zementmörtel verlegten Kacheln aus Meissener Porzellan®. Die Herrscher-Parade reicht von Konrad von Wettin, Markgraf von Meißen (1098 o. 1099–1157) bis zu Georg, König von Sachsen (1832–1904).

35 Saxony margraves, earls, dukes, princes and kings from the House of Wettin are shown on the north wall of the "Long Walk" of the Royal Mews (Augustus Street). The "Procession of the Princes" completed in 1907 is the world's largest porcelainmural and was created with 25 000 Meissen porcelain® tiles seamlessly fitted to cement mortar. The regents' parade ranges from Konrad of Wettin, Margrave of Meissen (1098 or 1099–1157) to Georg, King of Saxony (1832–1904).

Renaissance-Stallhof (1591 fertiggestellt) mit zwei 6,10 Meter hohen Bronzesäulen für das Ringstechen. Bis zur Mitte des 18. Jahrhunderts wurden hier u. a. Turniere und Hetzjagden veranstaltet. Der „Lange Gang" mit 20 toskanischen Säulen (oberhalb die Wappen wettinischer Lande und eine Sonnenuhr von 1568) verbindet Georgentor und Johanneum.

Renaissance Royal Mews (completed 1591) with two 6.10 meters high bronze pillars for the Ringstechen (a medieval game competition where a rider has to collect rings from the bronze post – the first one to collect all the rings is the winner). Tournaments and hunts, among others, were held here right up to the middle of the 18th century. The "Long Arcade", consisting of 20 Tuscan columns and featuring the House of Wettin coat-of-arms and a 1568 sundial above it, connects the Georgentor to the Johanneum.

Einer der schönsten Plätze Deutschlands, der Neumarkt zu Dresden mit der weltberühmten Frauenkirche, erstrahlt heute wieder in altem Glanz. Links die 2006 fertiggestellte Ladenpassage (drei Etagen) „Quartier an der Frauenkirche". Das Gebäude-Ensemble beherbergt auch Wohnungen, Geschäftsräume, ein Hotel und die Erlebniswelt der Glashütter Uhrenmanufaktur „A. Lange & Söhne". Die Sandsteinfigur im Vordergrund gehört zum „Türkenbrunnen".

One of the most beautiful squares in Germany, the Neumarkt (New Market) in Dresden together with the world-famous Frauenkirche, has now been restored to its former glory. The "Quartier an der Frauenkirche", a three-storey shopping mall on the left, was completed in 2006. The building complex also houses apartments, offices, a hotel and the wonderful showroom of the Glashütte watchmaker "A. Lange & Sons". The sandstone figure in the foreground is part of the "Turkish fountain".

An den Sieg des Kurfürsten Johann Georg III. (1647–1691) über türkische Truppen vor Wien erinnert dieser Brunnen. In der Mitte des achteckigen Sandsteintroges reckt sich Göttin Victoria. Das "Johanneum"- Palais dahinter mit der markanten doppelläufigen englischen Treppe geht auf König Johann (1801–1873) zurück. Seit 1956 dient es als Verkehrsmuseum.

This well was built to commemorate the victory of Elector Prince Johann Georg III (1647–1691) over the Turkish troops at the gates of Vienna. The goddess Victoria is seen rising in the middle of the octagonal sandstone trough. Behind that is the Johanneum palace with its distinctive double-barrelled English staircase, which can be traced back to King Johann (1801–1873). It has served as the transport museum since 1956.

Rund um den noblen Neumarkt sind Hotels verschiedener Kategorien zu finden. Vor dem 2006 eröffneten „Steigenberger Hotel de Saxe" steht das Denkmal für König Friedrich August II. (1797–1854). Der Monarch starb nach dem Schlag eines Pferdehufes in den Tiroler Alpen.

Around the elegant Neumarkt can be found hotels of varying categories. In front of the Steigenberger Hotel de Saxe opened in 2006 stands the monument to King Friedrich August II (1797–1854). The monarch died after being struck by a horse's hoof in the Tyrolean Alps.

Das faszinierende Spannungsfeld zwischen höfischer und bürgerlicher Baukunst spiegelt sich auch an diesem Quartier des Neumarktes zwischen Salzgasse und Rampischer Straße wider. Rechts vom „Coselpalais" (linker Bildrand) gruppieren sich drei Bürgerhäuser mit völlig unterschiedlicher Fassadenstruktur. Beeindruckend sind vor allem Balkon-Erker und barocker Ornament-Reichtum des Bürgerhauses direkt an der Rampischen Straße.

The fascinating tension between courtly and bourgeois architecture is also reflected in this quarter of the Neumarkt between Salzgasse and Rampischer Strasse. To the right of the "Cosel Palais" (left in the photo) is a grouping of three town houses with completely different facades. The most striking features are the corner bay window balconies and the ornamental Baroque richness of the town houses directly on the Rampische Strasse.

Wer heute die in alter Schönheit aufgebauten Wunder der Architektur des Neumarktes bestaunt und vor der am 30. Oktober 2005 wieder geweihten Dresdner Frauenkirche verweilt, ahnt kaum, welche Flammenhölle hier am 13. und 14. Februar 1945 herrschte. 772 Bomber entfachten mit 3500 Tonnen Bomben in zwei Angriffswellen ein Inferno, in dem mindestens 25 000 Menschen starben.

Whoever gazes at the beauty and architectural marvel of the resurrected Neumarkt and lingers in front of the Frauenkirche, newly consecrated on 30th October 2005, might hardly imagine what inferno raged here on 13th and 14th February 1945. In two waves of attacks, 772 bombers unleashed 3500 tons of bombs which created an inferno that killed at least 25 000 people.

Gottesdienst in der Frauenkirche. Zwischen 1726 und 1743 auf uraltem heiligen Grund errichtet (ein hölzerner Vorgänger existierte schon vor 1000 Jahren), ist die Frauenkirche Dresden die prachtvollste Kathedrale der evangelischen Christenheit. Sie verfügt heute über 1833 Sitzplätze. Das Haus ohne eigene Gemeinde ist begehrt für Taufen und Hochzeiten sowie bekannt für herausragende Konzerte.

A service at the Church of Our Lady. Built between 1726 and 1743 on ancient sacred ground (a wooden predecessor existed here 1000 years before), the Frauenkirche in Dresden is the most magnificent cathedral of Protestant Christianity. Today it provides seating for over 1833 visitors. The church does not have its own diocese, but nevertheless is in great demand for weddings and baptisms, and is also renowned for its outstanding concerts.

Weltweit gilt der Wiederaufbau der Frauenkirche als einzigartig. Die 197,7 Millionen Euro trugen über eine Million Spender zusammen. Der US-amerikanische Biochemiker Günter Blobel (geb. 1936) gab 820 000 Euro des Preisgeldes seines Nobelpreises von 1999. Das 4,60 Meter hohe Kreuz stiftete England. Königin Elisabeth II. (geb. 1926) spendete einen vierstelligen Betrag. Am Kreuz arbeitete der Londoner Kunstschmied Alan Smith (geb. 1948), dessen Vater mit seiner 57. Lancaster-Staffel 1945 Dresden vernichtete.

The reconstruction of the Frauenkirche is seen as unique, worldwide. Over one million donors contributed the sum of 197. 7 million euros. Günter Blobel, an American bio-chemist (born 1936) who won the Nobel Prize in 1999 donated 820 000 euros of his monetary award. England donated the 4.60-meter-high cross. Queen Elizabeth II (born 1926) also donated a four-figure sum. Alan Smith, a blacksmith whose father was a member of the 57th squadron which took part in the destruction of Dresden in 1945, worked on the cross.

Der 44. US-Präsident, Barack Obama (geb. 1961), besuchte am 5. Juni 2009 die Frauenkirche. In seiner Begleitung (v. l.): Kirchenbau-Direktor i. R. Dr.-Ing. E. h. Eberhard Burger (geb. 1943), Bundeskanzlerin Angela Merkel (geb. 1954), Pfarrer Holger Treutmann (geb. 1963), Landesbischof Jochen Bohl (geb. 1950), Sachsens Ministerpräsident Stanislaw Tillich (geb. 1959), Pfarrer Sebastian Feydt (geb. 1960).

The 44th U.S. President Barack Obama (born 1961) visiting the Frauenkirche on 5ᵗʰ June 2009. Accompanying him are (from left): Project Manager i. R. Dr.- Ing Eberhard Burger (born 1943), Federal Chancellor Angela Merkel (born 1954), Pastor Holger Treutmann (born 1963), Bishop Jochen Bohl (born 1950), the Prime Minister of Saxony Stanislaw Tillich (born 1959) and Pastor Feydt Sebastian (born 1960).

Altar und Orgel der Frauenkirche. Über dem zwölf Meter hohen und fast zehn Meter breiten Altar, welcher mit einem plastischen Bild „Die Historie von Christo am Ölberge" darstellt, ist der barocke Prospekt der Orgel zu sehen. Statt der im Feuersturm verglühten Silbermann-Orgel hat man ein modernes Instrument mit vier Manualen, 67 Registern und 4790 klingenden Pfeifen eingebaut.

Altar and organ of the Frauenkirche. Above the twelve-meter high and nearly ten-meter wide altar, which depicts a sculptured scene of "The Story of Christ on the Mount of Olives", the prospect of the Baroque organ can be seen. The Silbermann organ, which was destroyed in the firestorm, was replaced by a modern instrument with four manuals, 67 registers and 4790 melodic pipes.

Altmarkt aus der Vogelperspektive (vom Turm der Kreuzkirche) mit den Nachkriegsbauten der Westseite und dem Kulturpalast an der Wilsdruffer Straße. Der im Stil der Bauhaus-Moderne von Wolfgang Hänsch (geb. 1929) entworfene Kulturpalast schließt seit 1969 die Nordseite des Altmarktes ab. Das Haus ist Heimat der 1870 als „Gewerbehausorchester" gegründeten Dresdner Philharmonie (115 Musiker).

Bird's eye view of the Old Market Square (from the tower of Church of the Cross) with the post-war buildings on the west side and the Palace of Culture on Wilsdrufferstrasse. The Palace of Culture, designed in the Bauhaus style by Wolfgang Hänsch (born 1929), has closed off the Altmarkt to the north since 1969. The building is home to the Dresden Philharmonic orchestra (115 musicians), which became the successor to the "Gewerbehausorchester", founded in 1870.

Seit 1434 findet zur Adventszeit der Dresdner Striezelmarkt, der wohl älteste deutsche Weihnachtsmarkt, auf dem Altmarkt statt. Rund um eine sächsische Fichte und die mit 14,62 Meter höchste Stufenpyramide bieten über 200 Händler u. a. erzgebirgische Volkskunst, Pulsnitzer Pfefferkuchen, Pflaumentoffel (Schornsteinfeger aus Backpflaumen) und den patentrechtlich geschützten Dresdner Christstollen an – einen Rosinenstollen, den nur 150 Bäcker herstellen dürfen!

The Dresden Striezelmarkt, probably the oldest German Christmas market, has had its home on the Altmarkt since 1434. Surrounding a Saxon spruce and, at 14.62 meters, the highest multi-level "pyramide", over 200 traders offer, amongst other products, Erzgebirge folk artifacts, Pulsnitzer gingerbread, Pflaumentoffel (chimney sweep figures made from dried plums), and the world famous Dresden Stollen, a patented raisin cake that may only be produced by 150 bakers!

Evangelische Kreuzkirche vor dem Lückenschluss an der südöstlichen Altmarktseite. Im 13. Jahrhundert stand hier schon eine römische Basilika. Seit 1964 ist das Gotteshaus mit über 3100 Sitzplätzen die offizielle Predigtkirche des evangelischen Landesbischofs von Sachsen. Die Aussichtsplattform des 94 Meter hohen Turmes ist über 256 Stufen zu erreichen.

The Protestant Church of the Cross on the southeast side of the Old Market Square before the gap was closed. In the 13th century there was already a Roman basilica here. Since 1964, the church, which seats more than 3100, has been the official location where, when visiting, the Protestant Bishop of Saxony holds his sermons. The observation platform of the 94-meter high tower can be reached by climbing its 256 steps.

In der Kreuzkirche singen unter ihrem 28. Kantor Roderich Kreile (geb. 1956) die 140 Sänger (9 bis 19 Jahre alt) des Kreuzchores. Vor fast 800 Jahren gegründet, ist er einer der weltweit berühmtesten Knabenchöre. Tourneen führen den Chor seit 1920 regelmäßig durch Deutschland und Europa, nach Nord- und Südamerika sowie Asien.

In the Church of the Cross, the Kreuzchor, consisting of 140 singers (aged 9 to 19 years) performing under the baton of the 28th cantor, Roderich Kreile (born 1956). Founded almost 800 years ago, this is one of the most famous boys' choirs world-wide. It has been on tour regularly throughout Germany and Europe as well as North and South America and Asia since 1920.

Vom Turm der Kreuzkirche bietet sich dieser Blick auf das 10 000 Quadratmeter große Areal des 1905/10 errichteten Neuen Rathauses. Den Abschluss des 100,2 Meter hohen Turmes (Aussichtsplattform in 68 Meter Höhe, Zifferblatt der Uhr 4,25 Meter Durchmesser) bildet der goldene Rathausmann (5,05 Meter groß). Die vergoldete Skulptur aus Kupfer symbolisiert den Schutzpatron Herkules, dessen erhobene Hand auf Dresdens Schönheit weist.

From the tower of the Church of the Cross, one has a view over the 10 000 square meter area of the new City Hall built between 1905/10. On the top of the 100.2 meters tower (the observation platform is at a height of 68 meters, the clock face is 4.25 meters in diameter) stands the golden Rathausmann (5.05 meters high). The gilded copper sculpture symbolizes the patron Hercules whose raised arm greets beauteous Dresden.

Linke Seite: „Balkon Europas" – so nennt der Dresdner die Brühlsche Terrasse mit dem Terrassenufer, an dem die zur Sächsischen Dampfschifffahrt gehörende größte Raddampferflotte der Welt anlegt. Die in abendlicher Stimmung zu sehende Flaniermeile in rund zehn Meter Höhe ist 500 Meter lang und zwischen 20 und 200 Meter breit.

Left side: The river bank adjoining the Brühl Terrace, popularly known as the "Balcony of Europe", is where the largest paddle wheel steamer fleet in the world, a member of the Saxon Steam shipping Company, docks. The terrace promenade seen here in the evening atmosphere is about 10 meters high, 500 meters long and between 20 meters and 200 meters wide.

Eine jener schönen Blickbeziehungen, die sich von der Brühlschen Terrasse aus bieten. Über eine Treppenanlage gelangt man zum Neumarkt. Das Denkmal zeigt den Architekten Gottfried Semper (1803–1879).

One of those beautiful visual relationships that can be enjoyed from Brühl's Terrace. The staircase at the back leads to the Neumarkt. In the foreground is a monument showing the architect Gottfried Semper (1803–1879).

1894 wurde das Ensemble von Kunstausstellungsgebäude (links) und Kunstakademie (Hochschule für Bildende Künste Dresden) eingeweiht. Einer der ersten Direktoren der 1764 gegründeten Akademie war Giovanni Battista Casanova (1728–1795), der Bruder des Abenteurers Giacomo Casanova (1725–1798). Mit der Hochschule sind Namen wie Canaletto (1722–1780), Caspar David Friedrich (1774–1840), Otto Dix (1891–1969), Oskar Kokoschka (1886–1980) oder Eberhard Havekost (geb. 1967) verknüpft.

The ensemble consisting of the Art Exhibition Building (left) and the Academy of Fine Arts of Dresden was inaugurated in 1894. One of the first directors of the academy, which was founded in 1764, was Giovanni Battista Casanova (1728–1795), the brother of the adventurer Giacomo Casanova (1725–1798). Famous names such as Canaletto (1722–1780), Caspar David Friedrich (1774–1840), Otto Dix (1891–1969), Oskar Kokoschka (1886–1980) and Eberhard Havekost (born 1967) have all been associated with the Academy.

Die Augustusbrücke in der Abendsonne. Wo heute Dresdens älteste Flussquerung Altstadt und Neustadt verbindet, befand sich schon 1285 eine aus Stein gemauerte Brücke. Mit 24 Bögen, 561 Meter Länge und 8,5 Meter Breite gehörte sie zu den größten Brücken im damaligen Europa.

The Augustus Bridge in the evening sunlight. Dresden's oldest river crossing, linking the old part and the new part of the city of Dresden, was in 1285 originally a stone masonry bridge. With 24 arches, 561 meters long and 8.5 meters wide, it was among the largest bridges in the Europe of that time.

Kronentor und Langgalerien des Zwingers bei Nacht. Kurfürst Friedrich August I. (1670–1733) konzipierte diese europaweit einmalige Anlage als Festplatz für Ritterspiele und Lustbarkeiten des Hofes wie Bälle, Opern und Komödien, Damen-Rennen oder Schlittenfahrten.

The Crown Gate and the Long Galleries of the Zwinger at night. Elector Frederick Augustus I (1670–1733) designed this complex, which is unique in Europe, as festival grounds for jousting tournaments and court festivities such as balls, operas and comedies, races for the ladies of the court and sleigh rides.

Zu den zauberhaften Bauten Dresdens gehört der weltberühmte Zwinger, der hier aus der Vogelperspektive zu sehen ist. Diese 1709/32 entstandene Krönung barocker Baukunst, dieses 107 mal 204 Meter große faszinierend filigrane Wechselspiel von Sandstein-Pavillons und Galerien ist das Werk des Architekten Matthäus Daniel Pöppelmann (1662–1736) und des Bildhauers Balthasar Permoser (1651–1732).

Here is a bird's eye view of the world famous Zwinger, one of the most charming building ensembles of Dresden. Erected between 1709 and 1732, this crowning glory of Baroque architecture spanning 107 x 204 meters with a fascinating filigree interrelationship of sandstone pavilions and galleries, is the oeuvre of the architect Matthäus Daniel Pöppelmann (1662–1736) and the sculptor Balthasar Permoser "(1651–1732).

Östlicher Zwingerteil am Postplatz mit Langgalerie, Porzellanpavillon (vorn), Stadtpavillon und Deutschem Pavillon. Hier befindet sich die Porzellansammlung der Staatlichen Kunstsammlungen.

Eastern part of the Zwinger at Postplatz together with Long Gallery, Porcelain Pavilion (foreground), City Pavilion and German Pavilion. The porcelain collection of the State Art Collections is housed here.

Von der oberen Galerie zwischen Stadtpavillon (Glockenspielpavillon) und Deutschem Pavillon (vorn rechts) blicken wir auf den Zwingerhof mit Wallpavillon und Französischem Pavillon (hinten rechts).

From the upper gallery between the City Pavilion (Carillon Pavilion) and the German Pavilion (foreground right), we can see the central area of the Zwinger with the Wall Pavilion and the French Pavilion (right background).

Die weltberühmte Sixtinische Madonna von Raffaelo Santi (1483–1520). Das 2,69 mal 2,01 Meter große Ölgemälde ist die Hauptattraktion der Galerie Alte Meister (über 700 ausgestellte Gemälde) im Zwinger. Zahlreiche Werke des 15. bis 18. Jahrhunderts, zu denen Arbeiten von Bernardo Bellotto, genannt Canaletto (1722–1780), Giorgione (1478–1510), Rembrandt (1606–1669), Tizian (um 1490–1576) und Jan Vermeer (1632–1675) gehören, begründeten den Ruhm der Sammlung.

The world famous Sistine Madonna by Raffaello Santi (1483–1520). The 2.69 meters x 2.01 meters oil painting is the main attraction of the Zwinger's Gallery of the Old Masters, where over 700 paintings are exhibited. Numerous paintings from the 15th to 18th century among them works by Bernardo Bellotto popularly known as Canaletto (1722–1780), Giorgione (1478–1510), Rembrandt (1606–1669), Titian (c. 1490–1576) and Jan Vermeer (1632–1675) established the fame of the collection.

„Weißes Gold" unter Baldachinen und einem Pavillon im chinesischen Stil in der Porzellansammlung. Dieses Museum im Zwinger gilt als eine der weltgrößten Expositionen chinesischer und japanischer Porzellane sowie von Erzeugnissen der 1710 gegründeten Königlichen Porzellanmanufaktur Meissen®.

"White Gold" under baldachins and a pavilion in the Chinese style in the Porcelain Collection. This museum in the Zwinger is understood to be one of the world's largest exhibitions of Chinese and Japanese porcelain as well as of products manufactured by the Royal Meissen porcelain® manufactory established in 1710.

Europas wohl schönste Oper, die 1871/78 durch Gottfried Semper (1803–1879) errichtet wurde. Davor das 1889 eingeweihte Reiterstandbild von Sachsen-König Johann (1801–1873) auf dem Theaterplatz. Hier feierten Stars wie Maria Cebotari (1910–1940), Tino Pattiera (1890–1966) oder Peter Schreier (geb. 1935) rauschende Erfolge. Unter den Dirigenten Ernst Edler von Schuch (1846–1914), Fritz Busch (1890–1951) und Karl Böhm (1894–1981) erlebte die Oper bis 1942 ihre legendäre Glanzzeit. Daran will jetzt Christian Thielemann (geb. 1959) wieder anknüpfen.

Easily Europe's most beautiful opera house, it was built by Gottfried Semper (1803–1879) between 1871 and 1878. In front of the opera house, on Theatre Square, stands the equestrian statue of King Johann of Saxony (1801–1873), which was inaugurated in 1889. Stars such as Maria Cebotari (1910–1940), Tino Pattiera (1890–1966) and Peter Schreier (born in 1935) celebrated resounding successes here. Up to 1942 the opera house experienced its legendary prime under the conductors Ernst Edler von Schuch (1846–1914), Fritz Busch (1890–1951) and Karl Böhm (1894–1981). Christian Thielemann (born 1959) now wants to continue in this tradition.

Linke Seite, kleine Abb.: Büste des Hofnarren Joseph Fröhlich (1694–1757). Der geniale Bildhauer Johann Gottlieb Kirchner (1706 – um 1768) modellierte sie 1730 aus Meissener Porzellan®.

Left side, inset picture: Bust of court jester Joseph Fröhlich (1694–1757). The brilliant sculptor Johann Gottlieb Kirchner (1706 – to 1768) modelled it in 1730 from Meissen porcelain®.

Blick ins obere Vestibül (Zwingerseite). Es erinnert mit seiner kreuzgratgewölbten Halle über ionischen Säulenpaaren an die Loggien des Vatikans und Paläste in Genua. Grüne, Marmor vortäuschende Schäfte der Säulen und Pilaster bilden einen eindrucksvollen Kontrast zu den in Violett und Ocker ausgemalten Wänden.

View into the upper vestibule (facing the Zwinger). With its groined vaulted hall supported by pairs of Ionic columns, it brings to mind the loggias of the Vatican and of palaces in Genoa. Green artificial marble columns and pilasters form a striking contrast to the walls painted in purple and ochre.

Oberes Rundfoyer, das Semper nach den Schlossgalerien des Barock konzipierte: mit seitlichen Vestibülen und frei vor die Wand gestellten ionischen Säulen in grünem Kunstmarmor sowie hellgrauen korinthischen Dreiviertelsäulen. Durch die Rundbogenfenster bieten sich reizvolle Sichten auf den Theaterplatz und die Elblandschaft.

Upper circular foyer of the Semper Opera House which Semper modelled after the Royal Baroque Castle's galleries: with side vestibules and free-standing Ionic columns in artificial green marble as well as light grey Corinthian three-quarter columns. The arched windows offer a beautiful view onto Theatre Square and the Elbe riverscape.

Das klassische Ballett „Dornröschen" an der Semperoper. Die Musik von Peter I. Tschaikowski (1840–1891) spielt die Sächsische Staatskapelle. Die Choreographie stammt vom kanadischen Ballettdirektor Aaron S. Watkin (geb. 1970), das Bühnenbild schuf Arne Walther (geb. 1971).

The classical ballet "Sleeping Beauty" at the Semper Opera House. The Saxon State Orchestra plays the music of Peter I. Tchaikovsky (1840–1891). The choreography is by the Canadian ballet director Aaron S. Watkin (born 1970), the stage set was created by Arne Walther (born 1971).

Szenerie vom vierten Rang auf Zuschauerraum und Bühne bei einem Konzert. Mitglieder der Sächsischen Staatskapelle sitzen vor dem Bühnenvorhang von Ferdinand Keller (1842–1922). Komponist Richard Strauss (1864–1949), der von dem Weltklasse-Orchester (heute 145 Musiker) neun seiner Werke uraufführen ließ, nannte die Staatskapelle „Wunderharfe".

View from the fourth balcony towards the auditorium and stage during a concert. Members of the Saxon State Orchestra are seated in front of the stage curtain designed by Ferdinand Keller (1842–1922). Composer Richard Strauss (1864–1949) who had the world-class orchestra (now 145 musicians) play at the world premiere of nine of his works referred to the Saxon State Orchestra as a "magical harp".

Eine Moschee mit 62 Meter hoher Kuppel nahe dem Stadtzentrum. 1909 ließ Fabrikant Hugo Zietz (1858–1927) das Gebäude für seine „Orientalische Tabak- und Cigarettenfabrik Yenidze" im pseudoorientalischen Stil erbauen. Architekt Martin Hammitzsch (1878–1945) wurde wegen dieser angeblichen Geschmacksverirrung aus der Reichsarchitektenkammer ausgeschlossen. Später wurde er rehabilitiert und heiratete 1936 Angela Hitler (1883–1949), die Halbschwester von Diktator Adolf Hitler (1889–1945).

A mosque with a 62 meter high cupola near the city centre? In 1909 Hugo Zietz had the building for his "Yenidze Oriental tobacco and cigarette factory" built in the pseudo-Oriental style. The building's architect Martin Hammitzsch (1878–1945) was excluded from the Chamber of Architects of the Third Reich because of this alleged lapse of good taste. He was later rehabilitated and married Angela Hitler (1883–1949), the half-sister of Dictator Adolf Hitler (1889–1945) in 1936.

Marmor-Skulpturengruppe „Die Zeit entführt die Schönheit" (um 1722) auf der Wiese vor dem Palais im Großen Garten – dem größten Park von Elbflorenz. Der Dresdner liebt die rund zwei Quadratkilometer große (1900 mal 900 Meter) grüne Lunge der Stadt. Ab 1676 angelegt, wurde er zum Garten von europäischem Rang.

Marble sculpture group, "Time Abducting Beauty" (c. 1722) on the lawn in front of the Palais in the Grosse Garten, the largest park of the "Florence of the North". The citizens of Dresden adore the "green lung" of the city, which is about 2 kilometers (1900 meters x 90 meters) in area. Created in 1676, it became a garden of European importance.

An Wolfgang Amadeus Mozart (1756–1791), der vom 12. bis 18. April 1789 auf Konzerttournee in Dresden Station machte, erinnert der Mozartbrunnen mit seinen drei weiblichen Figuren „Anmut", „Heiterkeit" und „Ernst" auf der Bürgerwiese. Bildhauer Hermann Hosaeus (1875–1958) schuf die vergoldeten Bronzen 1907 im Auftrag des Mozartvereins Dresden.

Situated on the "Bürgerwiese" (citizens' meadow) is the Mozart memorial fountain with its three female figures "Grace", "Cheerfulness" and "Seriousness", created in honour of Wolfgang Amadeus Mozart (1756–1791) who, during a concert tour, made a stopover in Dresden from 12th to 18th April 1789. The sculptor Hermann Hosaeus (1875–1958) created the gilded bronze figures in 1907 on commission of the Mozart Society of Dresden.

Die 1872 bis 1874 erbaute russisch-orthodoxe Kirche des Heiligen Simeon vom wunderbaren Berge nahe dem Hauptbahnhof zeugt von dem großen Interesse, das Russen Dresden entgegenbringen. Für die Kirche stiftete der Komponist Sergei Rachmaninow (1873–1943) die Gasheizung, hier ließ Schriftsteller Fjodor Dostojewski (1821–1881) seine Tochter Ljubow taufen. Zu den Gemeindegliedern zählten Anarchist Michail Bakunin (1814–1876) und Schriftsteller Iwan Turgenjew (1818–1883). Russlands Kaiser Alexander II. (1818–1881) betete hier im Juni 1875.

The Russian Orthodox Church of Saint Simeon of the Wonderful Hill was built in 1872/74 near the main railway station and bears witness to the great interest Russians have in Dresden. The composer Sergei Rachmaninoff (1873–1943) donated the gas heating system and Fyodor Dostoyevsky (1821–1881) had his daughter Lyubov baptised here. Among the members of the congregation were anarchist Mikhail Bakunin (1814–1876) and writer Ivan Turgenev (1818–1883). The Russian Emperor Alexander II (1818–1881) prayed here in June 1875.

Neue Synagoge der jüdischen Gemeinde Dresden von 2000/01. Der moderne, in sich gedrehte Bau ist am höchsten Punkt 21 Meter hoch und besteht aus über 3000 je 120 mal 60 mal 60 Zentimeter großen Betonwerksteinen. Jüdisches Leben ist in der Stadt seit dem Mittelalter nachweisbar. Heute leben in Dresden etwa 730 Juden, die meisten sind Aussiedler aus Russland und der Ukraine.

The new Synagogue built in 2000/2001 for the Jewish congregation of Dresden. The modern upwardly rotating construction is 21 meters at the highest point and was constructed with more than 3000 concrete blocks each measuring 120 centimeters x 60 centimeters x 60 centimeters. Jewish life has been in evidence in the city since the Middle Ages. Today, about 730 Jews, mostly emigrants from Russia and the Ukraine, live in Dresden.

Zu den wertvollsten Büchern der SLUB zählt die Maya-Handschrift, der sogenannte „Codex Dresdensis". Sie ist die schönste von vier noch existierenden Handschriften der untergegangenen Hochkultur Mittelamerikas. Die um 1230 von Priestern auf Rindenpapier gemalten Hieroglyphen enthalten u. a. astronomisches und kalendarisches Wissen und werden auch mit Weltuntergangs-Prophezeiungen in Verbindung gebracht.

Right side below: Among the most valuable books of the SLUB is the Maya manuscript, the so-called "Dresden Codex". It is the most beautiful of four surviving manuscripts of the lost civilization of Central America. The approximately 1230 hieroglyphics drawn on bark paper by priests, among others include astronomical and calendrical knowledge and are also associated with apocalyptic prophecies.

Der 1902/10 auf einer zum Hochwasserschutz extra aufgeschütteten Wiese von Architekt Hans Erlwein (1872–1914) mit 68 Gebäuden errichtete Schlachthof beherbergt heute die „Messe Dresden". Literarisch berühmt wurde der Schlachthof durch Kurt Vonnegut (1922–2007). Der amerikanische Kriegsgefangene überlebte hier das Inferno des 13./14. Februar 1945 und verarbeitete es in seinem Erfolgsroman „Schlachthof 5".

The slaughterhouse complex, consisting of 68 buildings, which was designed by the architect Hans Erlwein (1872–1914) in 1902/10, on a meadow protected against flooding by an artificial bank, is today home to the "Messe Dresden" (Dresden Trade Fair complex). The slaughterhouse achieved literary fame through Kurt Vonnegut (1922–2007). The American POW (prisoner of war) survived the inferno of 13th to 14th February 1945 in one of its buildings, and assimilated the experience in his successful novel "Slaughterhouse-Five".

Dieses wunderliche Häuschen ließ 1823 der russische Fürst Nikolai Abramowitsch Putjatin (1749–1830) in Kleinzschachwitz als Dorfschule bauen. Der Kammerherr am russischen Hof verließ nach einem Liebesskandal St. Petersburg und siedelte sich 1797 in Kleinzschachwitz an, das damals noch nicht zu Dresden eingemeindet war. Als Wohltäter, Philosoph und liebenswerter Sonderling ging er in die Annalen ein.

This whimsical cottage in Kleinzschachwitz was built in 1823 by the Russian Prince Nikolai Putyatin Abramovich (1749–1830) to serve as a village school. The chamberlain at the Russian court left St. Petersburg after a romantic scandal in 1797 and settled in Kleinzschachwitz, which had not yet been incorporated into the municipality of Dresden. He went down in the annals as a benefactor, philosopher and loveable oddball.

An den französischen General Jean Victor Marie Moreau (1763–1813) erinnert dieses 1814 nach einem Entwurf von Gottlob Friedrich Thormeyer (1775–1842) im Süden Dresdens (Räcknitzhöhe) geschaffene Denkmal. Mit den verbündeten Österreichern, Russen und Preußen kämpfte er als Generaladjutant von Zar Alexander I. (1777–1825) gegen Napoleon. Am 27. August 1813 zerschmetterte ihm bei der Schlacht von Dresden eine Kanonenkugel beide Beine. Wenige Tage nach der Amputation starb er in Böhmen.

This monument designed in 1814 by Friedrich Gottlob Thormeyer (1775–1813) and situated at Räcknitzhöhe in the south of Dresden is dedicated to the French General Jean Victor Marie Moreau (1763–1813). Allied with the Austrians, Russians and Prussians, he fought as an Adjutant General of Tsar Alexander I (1777–1825) against Napoleon. In the battle of Dresden on 27 August 1813 a cannon ball shattered both of his legs. He died in Bohemia a few days after they were amputated.

Seit 1736 auf dem Neustädter Markt stehend, zählt der Goldene Reiter zu den Wahrzeichen Dresdens. Die 1250 Kilogramm schwere Metallplastik (eiserne Stabkonstruktion, Hülle aus getriebenem Kupferblech, Vergoldung mit ca. 190 Gramm Blattgold) stellt Kurfürst Friedrich August I. (1670–1733) in der Art römischer Cäsaren dar.

Standing since 1736 on the Neustadt Market, the Golden Horseman is one of the landmarks of Dresden. The 1,250 kilogramms metal sculpture (iron rod construction, body made of beaten copperplate, gilding with about 190 grams of gold leaf) presents Elector Frederick Augustus I (1670–1733) in the manner of a Roman emperor.

Dresdner Neustadt: Im Vordergrund das 1727/31 erbaute Japanische Palais. Der Monumentalbau fasziniert u. a. durch 24 Chinesenhermen im Innenhof. August der Starke plante hier ein gigantisches Porzellan-Schloss für seine chinesischen und japanischen Schätze sowie die neuen Waren aus der Porzellan-Manufaktur Meissen®. Dahinter recken sich die 87,5 Meter bzw. 81 Meter hohen Türme der Ev.-Luth. Dreikönigskirche (1421 erstmals erwähnt) und der Ev.-Luth. Martin-Luther-Kirche (1887 geweiht).

Dresden Neustadt with the Japanese Palace built in 1727/31 is seen in the foreground. The monumental building fascinates the visitor, among others, with 24 Chinese figures in the inner courtyard. August the Strong planned a gigantic porcelain castle here for his Chinese and Japanese treasures as well as the new products from the Meissen® manufactory. In the background rise up the 87.5 meters and 81 meters high towers of the Evangelical-Lutheran Church of the Three Kings (first mentioned in 1421) and the Evangelical-Lutheran Martin Luther Church (consecrated in 1887), respectively.

Knaben mit Milchflaschen oder Kondensmilch-Dosen gehören zu den vielen liebevollen Details, mit denen der Laden und die sich anschließende Trinkhalle ausgeschmückt sind.

Boys with milk bottles or cans of evaporated milk are among the many lovely details which adorn the shop and the adjoining drinking hall.

Linke Seite: Als „schönstes Milchgeschäft der Welt" und Touristen-Attraktion gilt dieser 1892 an der Bautzner Straße 79 (Neustadt) eröffnete Laden. Er ist das letzte Zeugnis eines Molkerei-Imperiums, das Paul Gustav Leander Pfund (1849–1923) in Dresden gründete. 248,90 Quadratmeter handbemalte Majolikafliesen von Villeroy & Boch zeigen u. a. Motive der Milchwirtschaft und Fabelwesen.

Left side: This shop at Bautzener Strasse 79, opened in 1892 and a major tourist attraction, is described as "the most beautiful dairy shop in the world". It is the last witness of the dairy empire that Paul Gustav Leander Pfund (1849–1923) founded in Dresden. 248.90 meters of hand-painted majolica tiles from Villeroy & Boch display, among others, motifs of the dairy industry and mythical creatures.

In dieser Villa, Nordstraße 28 (Neustadt) – heute das städtische Kraszewski-Museum –, wohnte und arbeitete der polnische Schriftsteller Josef Ignacy Kraszewski (1812–1887) ab 1873. Der politische Emigrant lebte mehr als 20 Jahre im Dresdner Exil. Zu seinen etwa 240 Romanen und Erzählungen gehören auch verfilmte Werke, die sich Sachsen im 18. Jahrhundert widmen.

In this villa on Nordstrasse 28 in Neustadt, which today houses the Kraszewski Municipal Museum, Josef Ignacy Kraszewski (1812–1887) the Polish writer lived and worked from 1873 onwards. The political emigrant lived for more than 20 years in exile in Dresden. Among his approximately 240 novels and short stories there are also filmed works dedicated to Saxony in the 18th century.

Straße Am Grünen Zipfel mit eingeschossigen Reihenhäusern, die zur ersten deutschen Gartenstadtsiedlung Hellerau (Name seit 1938, 1950 nach Dresden eingemeindet) gehört. 1908 gründete der Tischler Karl Schmidt (1873–1948) diese als Reaktion auf die Industrialisierung. Bis zum Zweiten Weltkrieg umfasste die Siedlung schon 387 Häuser mit 1900 Einwohnern.

A street-view of one-storey terrace houses on "Am Grünen Zipfel" which have been part of Germany's first garden city and has been called Hellerau since 1938; it was incorporated into Dresden in 1950. In 1903 the carpenter Karl Schmidt (1873–1948) founded the city as a reaction to industrialisation. Up to World War II the settlement comprised 387 houses with 1900 inhabitants.

Das Festspielhaus Hellerau baute Heinrich Tessenow (1874–1950) in den Jahren 1911/12 für den Schweizer Tanzpädagogen Emile Jaques Dalcroze (1865–1950). Dieser gründete hier seine „Bildungsanstalt für Musik und Rhythmus". Heute bietet der Zentralbau mit Säulenportiken dem Europäischen Zentrum der Künste Hellerau und der weltberühmten Company von US-Choreograf William Forsythe (geb. 1949) eine Residenz.

Heinrich Tessenow (1874–1950) built the Hellerau Festival Hall for the Swiss dancing instructor Emile Jaques Dalcroze (1865–1950) in 1911/1912, where the latter founded his "School for Music and Rhythm". Today, the central building with its portico main entrance offers a permanent residence to the European Centre for the Arts and also to the world famous dance company of US choreographer William Forsythe (born in 1949).

Militärhistorisches Museum der Bundeswehr am Olbrichtplatz (Neustadt). Das 1873/1877 als Arsenalhauptgebäude der Albertstadt errichtete Gebäude wird seit 1914 u. a. als Armeemuseum genutzt. Daniel Libeskind (geb. 1946), US-Architekt polnischer Abstammung, verlieh dem bis Oktober 2011 in siebenjähriger Bauzeit (62,5 Millionen Euro teuer) veränderten Ensemble durch seinen dominierenden Metall-Keil ein neues Aussehen.

The Museum of Military History of the Bundeswehr (German Military) at Olbrichtplatz (Neustadt). The building, erected in 1873/1877, served as the main arsenal in Albertstadt and has, among others, also been used as an army museum since 1914. Daniel Libeskind (born in 1946), a US architect of Polish origin, afforded the building a new appearance with his altered ensemble featuring a dominant metal wedge. The seven-year building project was completed in October 2011 at a cost of 62.5 million euros.

Bogenschützen-Plastik am Königsufer zwischen Albert- und Carolabrücke. Schöpfer des Bronzegusses, der hier seit 1936 auf einem fünf Meter hohen Sandsteinsockel steht, war Ernst Moritz Geyger (1861–1941). Ursprünglich ersann er den Bogenschützen 1895 für den Park von Potsdam-Sanssouci.

Sculpture of an archer on the Königsufer (King's river bank), between the Albert Bridge and Carola Bridge. The bronze cast, which has been standing here on a 5 meters high sandstone base since 1936, was created by Ernst Moritz Geyger (1861–1941). He had originally intended the 1895 archer for the Park at Sanssouci in Potsdam.

Schiffe der Sächsischen Dampfschifffahrt elbaufwärts Richtung Waldschlösschenbrücke. Wegen dieser von der Mehrheit der Bürger geforderten neuen Flussquerung verlor Dresden im Jahre 2009 den erst 2004 erhaltenen Weltkulturerbe-Titel der UNESCO. Nahe dem weißen Gebäudekomplex am linken Elbufer befand sich an der Angelikastraße die Villa, in der Russlands Präsident Wladimir Putin (geb. 1952) in der Ex-DDR bis Februar 1990 für den russischen Geheimdienst (zuletzt als Oberstleutnant) arbeitete.

Ships of the Saxon Steamshipping Company travelling upstream towards the Waldschlösschen Bridge. Due to the fact that the majority of the citizens demanded a new river crossing, in 2009, Dresden was relieved of its UNESCO World Heritage title, which had just been awarded in 2004. Near the white building complex on the left side of the river bank, on Angelikastrasse the villa is seen where President Vladimir Putin (born in 1952) worked in the former GDR for the Russian Secret Service (KGB) up to February 1990 (lastly with the rank of lieutenant colonel).

Zwischen Elbe und Dresdner Heide recken sich seit Mitte des 19. Jahrhunderts die drei prachtvollen Elbhangschlösser auf den steilen Loschwitzer Hängen empor. Bauherren der Schlösser waren 1854/56 ein Preußen-Prinz, 1853 die Frau eines Hofmarschalls sowie 1859/61 ein Großkaufmann. Sie dienen heute u. a. als Veranstaltungsorte, beherbergen eine Kochschule, ein Hotel und Restaurants. Ihre Architektur versetzt den Betrachter in die Zeit der Renaissancepaläste bzw. sogar der Gotik zurück.

Between the Elbe river and the Dresden Heath there are three magnificent castles, prominently situated on the steep Loschwitz slopes since the mid-19th century. The builders of the castles (1859/61) were a Prussian prince (1854/56), the wife of a Hofmarschall (marshal to the court) as well as an entrepreneur (1859/61). Today the castles are used for events and exhibitions and also accommodate a school for gastronomy, a hotel and restaurants. Their architecture enables the viewer to hark back to the days of Renaissance palaces and even the Gothic period.

Unter der 1891/93 errichteten Loschwitzer Brücke, die Einheimische „Blaues Wunder" nennen, fährt der Schaufelraddampfer „Krippen" (Baujahr 1992). Die 3800 Tonnen schwere und 260 Meter lange Stahlbrücke über der Elbe verbindet die durch ihre zahlreichen Villen als besonders nobel bekannten Stadtteile Loschwitz und Blasewitz.

The paddle-wheel steamer named the "Krippen" (built in 1992) passing under the 1891/93 Loschwitz Bridge popularly called the "Blue Wonder". The 260 meters long steel bridge, weighing 3300 tons, links the suburbs of Loschwitz and Blasewitz, made especially elegant due to their numerous villas.

Das mit lustigen Sprüchen verzierte Fachwerk-Anwesen Grundstraße 26 wird wegen einer rot bemalten, stählernen Amsel auf der Laterne vor dem Schutzheiligen liebevoll „Rote Amsel" genannt. Schöpfer des Ensembles von Wohnhaus und Atelier war der Kunstmaler Eduard Leonhardi (1828–1905), der als „Maler des deutschen Waldes" bekannt ist. Heute befindet sich hier eine städtische Galerie.

The half-timbered building on Grundstrasse 26, which is decorated with humorous sayings, is popularly known as "The Red Amsel" because of a red painted, steel blackbird on the lantern located in front of the patron saint. Creator of the house and studio complex was the painter Edward Leonhard (1828–1905), renowned as "Painter of the German Forest". Today, the building houses a municipal gallery.

Seit 1895 verbindet die Standseilbahn mit 563 Meter Streckenlänge die Stadt-teile Loschwitz und Weißer Hirsch (95 Meter über dem Elbtal). Auf den Schie-nen fahren zwei durch ein 38 mm dickes Stahlseil verbundene Waggons. Da-bei zieht der talwärts fahrende Wagen den sich bergauf bewegenden auch durch zwei Tunnel. Wir sehen die Ausweichstelle auf dem Viadukt über der Grundstraße.

Since 1895, the 563 meters long funicular railway has connected the districts of Loschwitz and Weisser Hirsch (95 meters above the Elbe valley). Two wagons travel on rails connected by two 38 mm thick steel cables. In this way the car moving downhill also pulls the car moving uphill through two tunnels. Here, we can see the place for evasive manoeuvring on the viaduct over Grundstrasse

Blick von der Bergstation der ältesten Bergschwebebahn der Welt und ersten Seilbahn Europas für das Personentransport auf das „Blaue Wunder" und das Elbtal. Seit 1901 verbindet dieses voll funktionstüchtige technische Denkmal Loschwitz mit dem 84 Meter höher gelegenen Oberloschwitz. Die beiden Wagen (274 Meter Streckenlänge) hängen an Schienen, welche durch 33 Trag-joche gestützt werden.

View of the "Blue Wonder" and the Elbe valley from the hill station of the oldest suspension railway in the world and the first cable car for passenger transport in Europe. Since 1901, this fully functional technical monument has connected Loschwitz with the 84 meters higher Oberloschwitz. The two cars (274-meter track length) are attached to rails that are supported by 33 yoke-shaped columns.

Luftbild der einstigen königlichen Sommerresidenz Pillnitz. Ihr Aussehen verdankt die barocke Pracht-Anlage Matthäus Daniel Pöppelmann (1662–1736) und Zacharias Longuelune (1669–1748). Sie lieferten Kurfürst Friedrich August I., dem Starken (1670–1733), der 1720/21 die Bauarbeiten für das Wasserpalais an der Elbe befahl, die Entwürfe. Von 1769 bis 1918 war Pillnitz ständiger Sommersitz des Dresdner Hofes. Heute zählt es zur Schlösserverwaltung des Freistaates.

Aerial view of Pillnitz, the former royal summer residence. Thanks are due to Matthew Daniel Pöppelmann (1662–1736) and Zacharias Longuelune (1669–1748) for the splendid Baroque appearance of the ensemble. They provided the designs to Elector Frederick Augustus I the Strong (1670–1733), who commissioned the construction of the Water Palace on the Elbe in 1720/21. From 1769 to 1918 Pillnitz was the permanent summer residence of the Dresden court. Today it is administered by the Department of Palaces, Castles and Gardens of the Free State of Saxony.

Bergpalais von 1723/24. August der Starke, der sich direkt mit dem Kaiser von China und dem Maharadscha von Indien verglich, ließ das Gebäude vermutlich nach einem Stich des Torbaues vom Kaiserpalast in Peking ausführen. Durch farbige chinoreske Malerei mit Figuren, Pflanzen und Tieren fand die Chinamode hier ihre erste architektonische Manifestation.

The Hill Palace of 1723/24. August the Strong, who compared himself with the Emperor of China and the Maharajah of India, presumably had the building copied from an engraving of the Imperial Palace Gate construction in Beijing. On account of the colourful Chinoresque manner of painting figures, plants and animals, Chinese painting practices here found their first architectural manifestation.

Über diese im Fluss endenden Stufen gelangte die mit Prunkgondeln aus Dresden anreisende Hofgesellschaft ins 1723/24 fertiggestellte Wasserpalais. Die Idee zur Freitreppe dürfte in Venedig zu finden sein, das August der Starke als junger Prinz auf seiner Kavalierstour besuchte.

The courtiers, arriving from Dresden in magnificent gondolas, were able to disembark on the river steps, emerging from the river and fronting the Water Palace, which was completed in 1723/24. The idea for the river steps might have come from Venice, which August the Strong visited on his grand tour as a young prince.

Herbststimmung im Pillnitzer Schlosspark. Am Ende der 760 Meter langen Maillebahn-Allee (ihr Name leitet sich von einem kricketähnlichen Ballspiel ab) steht seit 1785 diese von einem Prager Meister aus Sandstein geschlagene Deckelvase. Zu ihrem Dekor zählen die als Schlangenschwänze gearbeiteten Henkel.

Autumn ambience in Pillnitz palace garden. A lidded sandstone vase created by a master sculptor from Prague has been standing at the end of the 760-meter-long avenue called Mailbahn (its name derives from a ball game similar to cricket) since 1785. Serpent shaped handles are among its prominent features.

Rote Gondel mit hornblasendem Tritonen unter ihrem Schutzbau im Pillnitzer Park. Kurfürst Friedrich August III. (1750–1827), seit 1806 König Friedrich August I., ließ sie um 1800 von einem Hamburger Schiffszimmermeister bauen. 13 Gondoliere versahen auf ihr Dienst.

Red gondola with horn-blowing triton under an especially designed shelter in Pillnitz Park. Elector Friedrich August III (1750–1827), since becoming King Friedrich August I in 1806, ordered the gondola's construction by a Hamburg ship carpenter around 1800. 13 gondoliers were needed to manage the boat.

In diesem Hosterwitzer Haus nahe Schloss Pillnitz verlebte der Komponist der deutschen Nationaloper „Der Freischütz" Carl Maria von Weber (1786 – 1826) die Sommer 1818, 1819 sowie 1822/24. Heute sind seine ehemaligen Wohnräume ein städtisches Museum.

The composer of the German national opera "Der Freischütz", Carl Maria von Weber (1786–1826), spent the summers of 1818, 1819 and 1822/24 in this Hosterwitz house near Pillnitz. Today his former living quarters house a municipal museum.

Linke Seite: Inmitten der Rebhänge des sieben Hektar großen Pillnitzer Königlichen Weinberges bettet sich das ev.-luth. Dorfkirchlein „Zum Heiligen Geist" (1725 geweiht) an der Weinbergslehne in die reizvolle Kulturlandschaft ein.

Left Side: Amid the wine growing slopes of the seven-acre Royal Vineyard of Pillnitz the small Lutheran village church of the "Holy Spirit" (consecrated in 1725) is nestling in the beautiful surrounding countryside at the lower edge of the vineyard.

„Maria am Wasser" ist der Name der malerisch an der Elbe gelegenen Ev.-Luth. Dorfkirche von Hosterwitz. Ihre Vorgängerbauten hatten sogar als Wallfahrtsstätten für Elbschiffer Bedeutung. 1704/1774 barock erweitert, ist das Gotteshaus heute eine bekannte Hochzeitskirche.

"Maria on the Water" is the name of the Evangelical Lutheran village church of Hosterwitz, picturesquely situated on the Elbe. Its predecessor buildings even had importance as pilgrimage sites for Elbe river skippers. The church, extended in the Baroque style from 1704 to 1774, is today a well-known wedding chapel.

Das märchenhafte Wasserschloss Moritzburg
Moritzburg – the fairytale water castle

Inmitten einer Wald- und Teichlandschaft liegt etwa 13 Kilometer nordwestlich von Dresden eines der schönsten barocken Jagdschlösser Mitteleuropas. Nach Kurfürst Moritz (1521–1553), der hier zwischen 1542 und 1546 einen Renaissance-Palast anlegen ließ, heißt das traumhafte Ensemble Moritzburg. Zum charakteristischen Element des hochadeligen Jagd-Domizils wurden die vier Rundtürme der einst wehrhaften Anlage. Sein jetziges Aussehen mit großer Freitreppe, aufgestockten Türmen, Putten auf den Balustraden und acht Teichhäusern verdankt das Wasserschloss (barocker Vierflügelbau) zwei Männern: Kurfürst Friedrich August I., dem Starken (1670–1733), der den Umbau befahl und seinem Architekten Matthäus Daniel Pöppelmann (1662–1736).

Im Schloss standen der königlichen Familie mehr als 100 Zimmer zur Verfügung. Zur prachtvollen Ausstattung zählten mit Blattsilber belegte, mit Goldlack und leuchtenden Farben bemalte Ledertapeten in 60 Räumen (in 13 Salons erhalten). Bis 1945 gehörte das Schloss zum Privatbesitz der sächsischen Königsfamilie. Heute betreut Sachsens Schlösserverwaltung das Areal mit 65 000 Quadratmeter großem Park und 388 500 Quadratmeter Wasserfläche, zu dem auch das Fasaneriegelände mit Fasanenschlösschen (erbaut 1770/76) sowie Mole, Hafen und Leuchtturm am Großteich (erbaut um 1776) gehören. Im rund 8300 Einwohner zählenden Ort Moritzburg, der an die Schmalspurbahn Radebeul-Ost – Radeburg angebunden ist, befindet sich auch das Landgestüt Moritzburg der Sächsischen Gestütsverwaltung (Pferdezucht seit 1828).

In the midst of forests and lakes, about 13 kilometers north-west of Dresden, lies one of the most beautiful Baroque hunting lodges of Central Europe. The beautiful palace of Moritzburg is named after Elector Moritz (1521–1553) who had a Renaissance castle built here between 1542 and 1546. The four round towers of the once-fortified structure have become the characteristic elements of the aristocratic hunting domicile. The water castle (Baroque four-wing building) owes its present appearance – the large staircase, the storied/stacked towers, putti on the balustrades and eight lakeside houses – to two men: Elector Frederick Augustus I the Strong (1670–1733), who commissioned the conversion and his architect Matthew Daniel Pöppelmann (1662–1736).

In the castle, more than 100 rooms were at the disposal of the royal family. To the splendid furnishings counted with silver leaf, gold lacquer and leather wall-coverings painted in bright colours in 60 rooms (still remaining in 13 salons). Up to 1945 the palace was under the private ownership of the Saxon Royal Family. Today, the Saxon Department of Castles, Palaces and Gardens administers the 65 000 square meters park and the 388 500 square meters lakes, to which belong among them also the small Pheasant Castle (built between 1770 to 1776) located in the Pheasant Park, as well as the pier, harbour and lighthouse overlooking the lake (built around 1776). The small town of Moritzburg with its approximately 8300 inhabitants which is connected to the Radebeul-Ost–Radeburg small gauge railway, is also the home of the Moritzburg Stud Farm of the Saxon Stud Farm Administration (stud started in 1828).

Die Moritzburg ist heute eins der eindrucksvollsten Staats-Museen. Seit Jahrzehnten zählt sie zu den zauberhaftesten Kulissen für Filmaufnahmen und Konzerte, ist ein Lieblings-Ausflugsziel der Dresdner und ein touristisches Highlight für alle Sachsen-Besucher. Bis 1945 im Besitz der Königsfamilie aus dem Hause Wettin, war das Schloss bereits damals an 150 Tagen im Jahr für öffentliche Besichtigungen zugänglich.

Nowadays, Moritzburg is one of the most impressive state museums. For decades, it has been one of the most enchanting backdrops for film making and concerts, a favourite destination for the citizens of Dresden, and a tourist attraction for all visitors to Saxony. Until 1945 in the possession of the royal family from the house of Wettin, the castle was even then accessible 150 days a year for public tours.

Luftaufnahme der barocken Schlossanlage Moritzburg mit ihren vier Ecktürmen von Süden. Auf der linken Seite reckt sich der Glockenturm der Kapelle empor. In den oberen Stockwerken des Mittelbaues befindet sich der Steinsaal. Der Palast ist von einer quadratischen Terrasse umgeben, die im Süden und Norden über je 38 Meter lange Apparaillen erreichbar ist. Die Schlossinsel ist mit Ufermauern befestigt, beherbergt acht Kavalierhäuser.

Aerial view from the south of the Baroque castle complex of Moritzburg Castle with its four corner towers. The chapel bell tower rises up on the left side. On the upper floors of the central block is the Stone Hall. The castle is surrounded by a square terrace which can be reached from the south and the north via elongated ramps of 38 meters in length. The Castle island is secured by retaining walls and accommodates eight courtier houses.

Rechte Seite: Nachtidylle um Schloss Moritzburg. Der benachbarte Wald wurde Im Oktober 1996 zum Ort elnes spektakulären Fundes. Ein Schatzsucher-Ehepaar hatte per Metalldetektor Teile eines im Januar 1945 vergrabenen Wettiner-Besitzes entdeckt. Die drei Kisten mit teilweise mittelalterlichen Preziosen im Wert von rund zehn Millionen Euro bekam das vormals regierende Königshaus zurück.

Right side: Idyllic night time scenery near Moritzburg Castle. A spectacular find was made in the locality of the adjoining forest in October 1996. A treasure hunting couple had, with the help of a metal detector, discovered some possessions belonging to the Wettin Royal Family, which had been buried there in January 1945. The three crates with partly medieval gems worth about ten million euros were returned to the formerly reigning royal family.

Im 11,8 Meter hohen Speisesaal bzw. Monströsensaal (Grundfläche 21,5 mal 10,6 Meter) – dem größten Saal des Schlosses – gehören 67 Jagdtrophäen zum Wandschmuck. Sie sind zwischen 250 und 400 Jahre alt.

In the 11.8 meters high banqueting hall (also called the "Monströsensaal") having an area of 21.5 meters x 10.6 meters – the largest hall of the castle – the walls are decorated with 67 hunting trophies. They are between 250 and 400 years old.

Nahe Schloss Moritzburg befindet sich das Fasanenschlösschen. Dieses 1770/76 errichtete Palais im chinoisen Stil gehört durch seine originale Ausstattung zu den wichtigsten Zeugen des sächsischen Rokoko. Auf dem Dachreiter steht eine plastische Chinesengruppe.

The Small Pheasant Castle is located near Moritzburg Castle. Due to its original features, this castle, built in 1770/76 in the chinoiserie style, is one of the most important witnesses of Saxon Rococo. A sculpture of a Chinese group adorns the roof ridge.

Eine historische Dampflokomotive zieht die Waggons der zur Sächsischen Dampfeisenbahngesellschaft (SDG) zählenden Lößnitzgrundbahn durch die idyllische Teichlandschaft von Moritzburg. Seit 1884 verbindet diese Schmalspurbahn (Spurweite 750 mm) mit 16,4 Kilometer Streckenlänge die Städte Radebeul und Radeburg.

A historic steam locomotive pulls the wagons of the Lössnitzgrund train (belonging to the Saxon Steam Railway Company or SDG) through the idyllic landscape of the Moritzburg lakes. This narrow gauge railway (750 mm distance between rails) has been travelling the 16.4 kilometers distance between the towns of Radebeul and Radeburg since 1884.

Elbaufwärts — Schlösser, Uhren, Sächsische Schweiz
Upstream the Elbe river — castles, watches, Saxon Switzerland

Burgen, Schlösser und eine barocke Parkschöpfung, das Zentrum handwerklicher Uhrenherstellung sowie Sachsens Nationalpark voll bizarrer Felsen lassen sich elbaufwärts von Dresden erkunden. Zuerst begegnen wir einer der bedeutendsten Parkanlagen des Barock – Heidenau-Großsedlitz! Sachsens Kurfürst Friedrich August I. (1670–1733) plante hier ein zweites Versailles. Zur Vollendung fehlte ihm das Geld. Doch es entstand ein großartiges Gartenensemble mit Alleen, Terrassen und Treppen, Fontänen und Kaskaden, wertvollen Sandsteinfiguren und Orangerien. Unweit davon schlängelt sich Sachsens schönstes Tal, das Müglitztal, durch Gneis- und Porphyrfelsen sowie steile bewaldete Berghänge. Schloss Weesenstein von Sachsen-König Johann (1801 – 1873) oder so geheimnisvolle Adelssitze wie Dohna, Bärenstein, Lauenstein und Kuckuckstein machen den besonderen Reiz des 40 Kilometer langen Tales aus. Im Herzen befindet sich mit dem Städtchen Glashütte (4500 Einwohner) das Zentrum der deutschen Uhrenherstellung.

Weiter elbaufwärts Richtung Böhmen liegt Pirna (1233 erstmals urkundlich erwähnt) – eine der ältesten und schönsten Städte des oberen Elbtals mit etwa 40 000 Einwohnern. Pirna ist das Tor zu einer wildromantischen Landschaft mit Sandsteingipfeln, Felssäulen, stillen Waldtälern, tiefen Schluchten. Dem Elbsandsteingebirge gaben im 18. Jahrhundert Kunstmaler den Namen „Sächsische Schweiz". Zu den Perlen der Region zählt die Festung Königstein, die sich 240 Meter über der Elbe auf einem Tafelberg mit 9,5 Hektar großem Felsplateau erhebt.

Fortresses, castles and a Baroque park creation, the centre of craftsmanship and watch making as well as Saxony's National Park filled with its bizarre rocks – all can be explored going upstream river from Dresden.

First, we encounter one of the most important parks of the Baroque – Heidenau-Grosssedlitz. Here, Saxon Elector Friedrich August I (1670–1733) had planned a second Versailles. Though lacking the funds to complete it, yet he nevertheless managed to create a great garden ensemble with tree lined avenues, terraces and staircases, fountains and cascades, precious sandstone statues and orangeries. Not far from there, Saxony's most beautiful valley, the Müglitztal, winds through gneiss and porphyry rocks and steep wooded hillsides. Weesenstein Castle, built by Saxon King Johann (1801–1873), mysterious domiciles of the aristocracy such as Dohna, Bärenstein, Lauenstein and Kuckuckstein, all make up the special appeal of the 40-kilometer-long valley. At the heart of the Müglitztal is the town of Glashütte (4500 inhabitants), the centre of German watch making.

Further upstream, towards Bohemia, there is Pirna (first mentioned in 1233), one of the oldest and most beautiful cities in the upper Elbe Valley with about 40 000 inhabitants. Pirna is the gateway to a romantic landscape of sandstone peaks, rock pillars, quiet forest valleys and deep gorges. Artists first gave the name "Saxon Switzerland" to the Elbe Sandstone Mountains in the 18th century. Among the pearls of the region is the Königstein fortress built on top of a table mountain 9.5 hectares in area and rising 240 meters above the river Elbe.

Der vom sächsischen Kurfürsten für ein grandioses Schlossareal vorgesehene Barockgarten Großsedlitz in Heidenau (18 Hektar groß) beeindruckt bis heute durch die Weitläufigkeit seiner Anlage. Diese Luftaufnahme zeigt das Garten-Paradies vom unteren Orangerieparterre mit seinen Wasserspielen (unten links) bis zum oberen Teil mit dem Palais-Gebäude und dem Friedrichsschlösschen.

The Elector of Saxony, for a grand Baroque castle ground, provided Großsedlitz-Heidenau (18 hectares) to this day impressed by the vastness of its surroundings. This aerial photograph shows the garden paradise from the lower ground floor orangery with its water features (bottom left) to the upper part of the palace-castle and Friedrich's castle.

Auf einem Felsvorsprung über dem Tal der Müglitz reckt sich das 1318 erstmals erwähnte Schloss Weesenstein empor. Berühmtester Besitzer war der universell gebildete sächsische Prinz und spätere König Johann (1801–1873), welcher hier Dantes „göttliche Komödie" übersetzte und kommentierte. Heute ist das Schloss im Besitz des Freistaates Sachsen als Museum öffentlich zugänglich.

Weesenstein castle, first mentioned in 1318, can be seen stretching out over a promontory overlooking the Müglitz valley. The most famous owner was the universally educated Saxon Prince and later King Johann (1801–1873), who translated and annotated Dante's "Divine Comedy". Today the castle, which is open to the public as a museum, is owned by the Free State of Saxony.

Glashütte (seit 1506 Stadt- und Bergrecht) am Fuß des Osterzgebirges ist die deutsche Uhrenhauptstadt. 1845 begründete Ferdinand Adolph Lange (1815–1875) die tickende Tradition. Heute gibt's hier über ein Dutzend Uhren-Manufakturen wie A. Lange & Söhne, Glashütter Uhrenbetrieb GmbH, NOMOS Glashütte, Nautische Instrumente Mühle Glashütte GmbH oder Wempe Chronometerwerke.

Glashütte (city and mining charter since 1506) located at the foot of the eastern Erzgebirge, is the capital of the German watch making industry. In 1845 Ferdinand Adolph Lange (1815–1875) founded the "ticking" tradition. Today there are over a dozen watch manufacturers such as A. Lange & Söhne, Glashütte Uhrenbetrieb Ltd, NOMOS Glashütte, Mühle Glashütte (nautical instruments) Ltd. or Wempe chronometer works.

Meisterliche Handarbeit macht viele Glashütter Uhren so wertvoll.

Masterful handwork ensures the high value of many Glashütte wristwatches.

Das Rathaus von Pirna auf dem 90 mal 65 Meter großen Marktplatz. Ein Vorgängerbau existierte schon zum Ende des 14. Jahrhunderts. In der Stadt an der Elbe hat sich manches vom Gepräge vergangener Zeiten bewahrt. Dazu gehören auch die mächtige Ev.-Luth. Stadtkirche „St. Marien" (Baubeginn 1502), Häuser mit Sitznischenportalen, Fenstergewänden und Kellern aus gotischer Zeit.

Pirna Town Hall is situated on the 90 meters x 60 meters market place. An earlier building had already existed here at the end of the 14th Century. The character of past times has been wonderfully preserved in the city on the Elbe River. Examples of this include the mighty Lutheran City Church "St. Marien" (begun in 1502), buildings with seating niche portals, decorated window frames and basements from the Gothic period.

Malerisch liegt das Städtchen Königstein mit seinen rund 2300 Einwohnern am Bielatal in der Sächsischen Schweiz zwischen Festung (links) und Elbe. 1379 erstmals urkundlich erwähnt, geht der Name des Ortes auf die einst den böhmischen Königen gehörende Burg („auf dem Stein des Königs") zurück. Von 1961 bis 1990 wurde im Ort Uran für die sowjetischen Atombomben abgebaut.

Located in Saxon Switzerland in the Bielatal (Biela valley) between the fortress (on the left) and the River Elbe, the town of Königstein, with around 2300 inhabitants is truly picturesque. First mentioned in 1379, the name of the place ("on the stone of the king") can be traced back to the Bohemian kings who owned the castle. From 1961 to 1990, uranium was mined here for use in Soviet nuclear weaponry.

Die pittoreske Felsenwelt entstand aus einem Meer der Kreidezeit. Hier warten über 1100 Klettergipfel auf Bergsteiger aus aller Welt, sind rund 1200 Kilometer Wanderwege markiert, von denen der 112 Kilometer lange „Malerweg" der bekannteste ist. Eine 93 Quadratkilometer große Fläche des Elbsandsteingebirges gehört zum Nationalpark Sächsische Schweiz.

The picturesque area of rocky valleys and ridges originated from a sea in the Cretaceous period. Over 1100 peaks offer challenges to rock climbers from all over the world. In addition, there are about 1200 kilometers of sign-posted hiking trails, of which the 112-kilometer "Malerweg" (artist's way) is the best known. A 93-square-kilometer area of the Elbe Sandstone Mountains belongs to the Saxon Switzerland National Park.

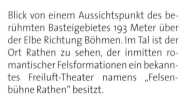

Blick von einem Aussichtspunkt des berühmten Basteigebietes 193 Meter über der Elbe Richtung Böhmen. Im Tal ist der Ort Rathen zu sehen, der inmitten romantischer Felsformationen ein bekanntes Freiluft-Theater namens „Felsenbühne Rathen" besitzt.

View towards Bohemia from a lookout point in the famous Bastei area 193 meters above the river Elbe. In the valley one can see Rathen, which boasts a well-known open-air theatre called "Felsenbühne Rathen" (Rathen amphitheatre) set in the midst of romantic rock formations.

Touristenmagnet: Auf dem Königstein erhebt sich 361 Meter über dem Meeresspiegel Europas größte Felsen-Festung. Durch 43 Meter hohe Mauern über Jahrhunderte uneinnehmbar sowie mit teilweise 400 Jahre alten Bauten, dem 152,5 Meter tiefen Brunnen (3,5 Meter Durchmesser), großen Kanonen und Kasematten ist sie fast vollständig erhalten.

A famous tourist attraction is Königstein, Europe's largest rock-fortress, soaring to a height of 361 meters above sea level. The complex, with its 43 meter high walls, was impregnable for centuries and is in an almost perfect state of preservation. It features 400 year old buildings, a 152.5 meters deep well (3.5 meters diameter), large guns and casemates.

Elbabwärts zu Wein, Indianern, Meissener Porzellan®
Downstream to local wine, Indians and Meissen porcelain®

Von ihrer heiteren, beschwingten Seite zeigt sich Dresdens Umgebung elbabwärts entlang der Sächsischen Weinstraße bis Diesbar-Seußlitz. Über weite Strecken bestimmen idyllische Elbdörfer und steile Rebhänge des nördlichsten und mit etwa 450 Hektar kleinsten Weinanbaugebietes Deutschlands (850 Jahre Tradition) die uralte Kulturlandschaft.

Direkt an die Landeshauptstadt schließt sich die Villen- und Gartenstadt Radebeul (1349 erstmals erwähnt, seit 1924 Stadt) mit ihren fast 34 000 Einwohnern an. Bereits um 1860 prägte sich für diesen reizvollen Landstrich der Begriff „Sächsisches Nizza". Hier wirkten so bekannte Persönlichkeiten wie der Abenteuerschriftsteller Karl May (1842–1912), dessen Witwe mit dem Artisten Patty Frank (1876–1959) den Grundstein für eine der wertvollsten ethnologischen Sammlungen zur Kultur der nordamerikanischen Indianer in Europa legte. In Radebeul befindet sich auf dem Gelände eines barocken Landsitzes auch das 2002 als Erlebnisweingut umgestaltete „Sächsische Staatsweingut Schloss Wackerbarth".

Am Ausgang des Elbtalkessels liegt rund 25 Kilometer nordwestlich von Dresden die über 1000-jährige Stadt Meißen (rund 27 500 Einwohner). Bereits 929 legte hier der deutsche König Heinrich I. (876–936) auf dem Burgberg ein befestigtes Militärlager an. Die mittelalterliche Stadt ist durch ihren Dom, die Albrechtsburg und vor allem die Staatliche Porzellanmanufaktur Meissen GmbH berühmt. Seit 1710 wird hier das berühmte Meissener Porzellan® hergestellt.

Downstream the environs of Dresden show themselves at their most cheerful, up-beat side along the Saxon Wine Route all the way to Diesbar-Seusslitz. Over long distances, idyllic Elbe villages and steep slopes determine the cultural landscape of the northernmost and, with its approximately 450 hectares of vineyards, the smallest wine-growing region of Germany (850 year old tradition). The villa and garden city of Radebeul (first mentioned in 1349, it achieved city status in 1924) with its approximately 34 000 inhabitants borders directly on the state capital. Already in 1860 the nickname "Saxon Nice" was coined for this delightful region. In this area lived and worked well-known personalities such as the adventure writer Karl May (1842–1912), whose widow, together with the artist Patty Frank (1876–1959), laid the foundation for one of Europe's most valuable ethnological collections of the culture of North American Indians. Also located in Radebeul is the "Sächsische Staatsweingut Schloss Wackerbarth" (Saxon State Winery Wackerbarth Castle) redesigned for a "winery experience" in 2002 on the site of a former Baroque country.

About 25 kilometres northwest of Dresden at the end of the Elbe valley basin lies the 1000-year-old town of Meissen (around 27 500 inhabitants). Already in 929 German King Heinrich I (876–936) set up a fortified military camp on the fortress hill. The medieval city is famous for its cathedral, the Albrechtsburg palace and especially the Meissen® State Porcelain Manufactory Ltd. Since 1710, the world famous Meissen porcelain® has been manufactured here.

Achteckiges Belvedere zwischen dem oberen Garten und den terrassierten Rebhängen vom „Staatsweingut Schloss Wackerbarth". Das imposante Ensemble, zu dem auch ein Barock-Schloss und die Kellerei gehören, schuf sich 1727/31 Generalfeldmarschall August Christoph Graf von Wackerbarth (1662–1734) als Alterssitz.

Octagonal belvedere between the upper garden and the terraced vineyards of "Schloss Wackerbarth State Winery". The imposing ensemble, which also includes a Baroque castle and winery, was created in 1727/31 by Field Marshal August Christoph Graf von Wackerbarth (1662–1734) as his retirement home.

Weinlese von Hand auf dem Radebeuler Wackerbarth-Rebhang. Der fruchtbare Boden des Elbtals lässt rund 40 verschiedene Rebsorten gedeihen. Darunter großartige Weine wie Grauburgunder und Traminer, Spätburgunder und Dornfelder. Zu den Hauptrebsorten des Anbaugebietes, das nur 0,2 Prozent der deutschen Weinmenge ausmacht, zählen Müller-Thurgau, Riesling und Weißburgunder.

Harvest by hand on the Wackerbarth vineyard in Radebeul. The fertile soil of the Elbe Valley can grow about 40 different varieties, including great wines such as Pinot Gris, Traminer, Pinot Noir and Dornfelder. Among the main varieties of the cultivating region, which accounts for only 0.2 percent of German wine production, are Muller-Thurgau, Riesling and Pinot Blanc.

Rechte Seite oben: „Villa Bärenfett" des Radebeuler Karl-May-Museums (eröffnet 1928). Die gleichnamige Stiftung erinnert an den erfolgreichsten deutschsprachigen Abenteuerschriftsteller Karl May (1842–1912), der mit Gestalten wie „Winnetou" und „Old Shatterhand" Generationen begeisterte. Gleichzeitig wird eine international hoch geachtete Sammlung zum Leben der Indianer präsentiert.

Right side above: "Villa Bärenfett" of the Karl May Museum in Radebeul (opened in 1928). The foundation of the same name highlights the most successful German adventure writer Karl May (1842–1912) who inspired generations of readers with characters like "Winnetou" and "Old Shatterhand". Simultaneously, an internationally highly esteemed collection of Indian life may also be viewed.

Diorama „Heimkehr von der Schlacht" in der Ausstellung „Indianer Nordamerikas". Mehr als 800 Original-Exponate wie diese aus dem 18. und 19. Jahrhundert zeigen hervorragend das Alltagsleben der Indianer und machen die völkerkundliche Schau des Karl-May-Museums einzigartig.

Diorama "Return from the battlefield" in the "Native Americans" exhibition. More than 800 original exhibits such as these from the 18th and 19th century brilliantly display the everyday life of the Indians and render the ethnographic exhibition of the Karl May Museum unique.

Vom Turm der Meißener Frauenkirche bietet sich das traumhafte Panorama über den Marktplatz und die engen Gassen der Stadt auf den Bergsporn mit Dom und Albrechtsburg, die den Wettinern kurzzeitig als Residenz diente. Der Ev.-Luth. Dom St. Johannes Evangelista und Donatus ist das bedeutendste Bauwerk des Mittelalters in Sachsen.

The view from the tower of the Meissen Frauenkirche offers a magnificent panorama over the market place and the narrow lanes of the city onto the mountain spur with the cathedral and the Albrechtburg palace which for a short time, served as the Wettin residence. The Lutheran Cathedral of St. John the Evangelist and St. Donat is the most important monument of the Middle Ages in Saxony.

Blick von der Juchhöhe auf die von grünen Hängen gesäumte über 1000-jährige Domstadt Meißen mit dem Burgberg an der Elbe. Hier ist die Wiege Sachsens, wurde der Freistaat im Jahre 1990 wieder gegründet.

View from the verdantly lined slopes of the Juchhöhe over the 1000-year-old cathedral city of Meissen together with the fortress hill on the Elbe. Here is the "Cradle of Saxony", where the Free State was re-established in 1990.

Übergang vom 2005 errichteten Besucherzentrum zur 1916 eröffneten Schauhalle des Museum of Meissen Art® der Manufaktur Meissen®. Am 7. März 1710 von Kurfürst Friedrich August I. (1670–1733) gegründet, ist sie die traditionsreichste Manufaktur Europas und seit über 300 Jahren das Mekka für Liebhaber des handgefertigten Luxus.

Crossing from the Meissen® manufactory's visitor's centre (built in 2005) to the Museum of Art® exhibition hall opened in 1916. Founded by Elector Frederick Augustus I (1670–1733) on 7th March 1710, it has been the porcelain manufactory with the richest tradition in Europe and the Mecca for collectors of handmade luxury for over 300 years.

Staffage des Eulenspiegels in der Malerei. In der Manufaktur Meissen® werden alle Dekore von hoch talentierten Malern per Hand auf das Porzellan gemalt. Selbst das Rohkaolin, die Porzellanerde, kommt aus dem manufaktureigenen Bergwerk in Seilitz bei Meißen.

Staffage of Eulenspiegel in porcelain painting. In the Meissen® manufactory all the decors are hand-painted on porcelain by highly talented artists. Even the raw kaolin used in porcelain production comes from the manufactory's own mine in Seilitz near Meissen.

Terrine des Schwanenservice mit Galatea. Sie gehört zu einem Prachtservice, welches aus über 2200 einzelnen Geschirrteilen besteht und heute noch komplett lieferbar ist. Die Modelle hierfür schuf der geniale Johann Joachim Kaendler (1706–1775) im Jahre 1740.

Tureen of the Swan Service with Galatea. It belongs to a magnificent tableware service, which consists of over 2200 individual crockery pieces and is still available in complete sets. The models for it were created by the brilliant Johann Joachim Kaendler (1706–1775) in the year 1740.

Barockschloss Seußlitz in Diesbar-Seußlitz. Ein erstes Landschloss ließ hier bereits Markgraf Heinrich der Erlauchte (vor 1216–1288) um 1250 bauen. Später stiftete er es den Klarissen als Nonnenkloster. Das jetzige Schloss (privater Besitz) wurde nach 1722 von Graf Heinrich von Bühnau (1697–1762) durch den Dresdner Frauenkirchen-Erbauer George Bähr (1666–1738) errichtet.

Seusslitz Baroque Castle in Diesbar-Seusslitz. A first rural castle had already been built here for Margrave Heinrich the Illustrious (circa 1216 to 1288) in 1250. He later donated it to the Poor Clare Nuns as a convent. The present castle (in private ownership) was built for Count Heinrich von Bühnau (1697–1762) by the Dresden Frauenkirche architect George Bähr (1666–1738) after 1722.

Wer entlang der Weinstraße elbabwärts wandert, stößt im Weindorf Zadel vor der Ev.-Luth. St. Andreas-Kirche (Vorgängerbau seit Ende des 12. Jahrhunderts, Neubau 1842 geweiht) auch auf solch eine Gänseherde.

Hiking the wine route downstream – one may encounter such a flock of geese in the wine village of Zadel in front of St. Andrew's Lutheran Church (originally built in the 12th century, the new building was inaugurated in 1842).

Quellen/Bibliography

Blaschke, Karlheinz (Hrsg.): Geschichte der Stadt Dresden. Band 1. Von den Anfängen bis zum Ende des Dreißigjährigen Krieges. – Theiss Stuttgart 2005

Dehio, Georg: Handbuch der deutschen Kunstdenkmäler. Sachsen I Regierungsbezirk Dresden. – Deutscher Kunstverlag München 1996

Dietrich, Andrea (Hrsg.): Der Große Garten zu Dresden – Gartenkunst in vier Jahrhunderten. – Sächsische Schlösserverwaltung Michael Sandstein Dresden 2001

Donath, Matthias: Sächsisches Elbland. Kulturlandschaften Sachsens. – Edition Leipzig Leipzig 2009

Hartmann, Hans-Günther: Schloß Pillnitz. Verlag der Kunst Dresden 1991

Helas, Volker: Architektur in Dresden 1800 – 1900. – Verlag der Kunst Dresden 3. Auflage 1991

Helfricht, Jürgen: Astronomiegeschichte Dresdens. – Hellerau Dresden 2001

Helfricht, Jürgen: Die Dresdner Frauenkirche. Eine Chronik von 1000 bis heute. – Husum Verlag Husum, 7., aktualisierte Auflage 2010

Helfricht, Jürgen: Die Synagoge zu Dresden. – Tauchaer Verlag Taucha 2001

Helfricht, Jürgen: Die Wettiner – Sachsens Könige, Herzöge, Kurfürsten und Markgrafen (Taschenlexikon). – Sachsenbuch Leipzig 4. aktualisierte Auflage 2007

Helfricht, Jürgen: Das Königliche Dresden. – Husum Verlag Husum 2011

Helfricht, Jürgen: Dresden und seine Kirchen. – Evangelische Verlagsanstalt Leipzig 2005

Helfricht, Jürgen: Dresdner Kreuzchor und Kreuzkirche. Eine Chronik von 1206 bis heute. – Husum Verlag Husum 2004

Helfricht, Jürgen: Kleines ABC des Meissener Porzellans®. – Husum Verlag Husum 2011

Helfricht, Jürgen: Kleines Dresden-ABC. – Husum Verlag Husum 2005

Helfricht, Jürgen: Sehnsucht nach dem alten Dresden. Zeitzeugen erinnern sich der unzerstörten Stadt. – Verlags- und Publizistikhaus Dresden 2005

Helfricht, Jürgen: The Dresden Frauenkirche – Church of Our Lady. A chronicle from 1000 A. D. to the present. – Husum Verlag Husum 2011

Helfricht, Jürgen: Traumblicke auf Dresden und das Elbtal. – Husum Verlag Husum 2007

Helfricht, Jürgen: Traumwege durch das alte Dresden. – Husum Verlag Husum 2007

Helfricht, Jürgen: Wahre Geschichten um Sachsens schönstes Tal. Tauchaer Verlag Taucha 2000

Helfricht, Jürgen: Zauberhaftes Dresden. Silhouetten von Elbflorenz. Husum Verlag Husum 2010

Kleineberg, Andreas u. a.: Germania und die Insel Thule. Die Entschlüsselung von Ptolemaios „Atlas der Oikumene". – Wissenschaftliche Buchgesellschaft Darmstadt 2010

Löffler, Fritz: Das alte Dresden. Geschichte seiner Bauten. – E. A. Seemann Leipzig 14. Auflage 1999

Löffler, Fritz; Pritsche, Willy: Der Zwinger. – E. A. Seemann Leipzig 5. Auflage 2004

Lupfer, Gilbert; Sterra, Bernhard; Wörner, Martin (Hrsg.): Architekturführer Dresden. – Dietrich Reimer Berlin 1997

Stimmel, Folke u. a.: Stadtlexikon Dresden A – Z. – Verlag der Kunst Dresden 1994

Syndram, Dirk: Das Schloß zu Dresden. Von der Residenz zum Museum. – Koehler & Amelang München Berlin 2001

Triebisch

Meißen

Moritzburg

Dr

Hellerau
Klotzsche

Radebeul

Albertstadt

Elbe

Innere
Neustadt

Blasewitz

Altstadt

Großer
Garten

Strehlen